To Anne

With all our good
wishes.

Ken + Chris

COTTAGE ANTIQUES

By Therle Hughes:

OLD ENGLISH FURNITURE
SMALL DECORATIVE ANTIQUES
MORE SMALL DECORATIVE ANTIQUES
ENGLISH DOMESTIC NEEDLEWORK, 1560–1860
SMALL ANTIQUES FOR THE COLLECTOR

By G. Bernard Hughes:

ENGLISH DOMESTIC SILVER, 1500–1820
ENGLISH GLASS FOR THE COLLECTOR, 1660–1860
ENGLISH AND SCOTTISH EARTHENWARE, 1660–1860
ENGLISH POTTERY AND PORCELAIN FIGURES

By Bernard and Therle Hughes:

ENGLISH PORCELAIN AND BONE CHINA, 1743–1850
SMALL ANTIQUE FURNITURE
ENCYCLOPAEDIA OF ENGLISH CERAMICS

Interior of a Yorkshire moorland cottage, as shown in
the Castle Museum, York.

THERLE HUGHES

COTTAGE ANTIQUES

LONDON
LUTTERWORTH PRESS

First published 1967
Second impression 1968

7188 0171 7

PRINTED IN GREAT BRITAIN BY
WILLIAM CLOWES AND SONS, LIMITED, LONDON AND BECCLES

TO
MY HUSBAND

CONTENTS

7

LIST OF PLATES

Interior of a Yorkshire moorland cottage, as shown in the
Castle Museum, York   *Colour frontispiece*

9

LIST OF PLATES

11

INTRODUCTION

COUNTRY cottages tend to be better furnished today than they have ever been. To our eyes the antique oak and gleaming brass, the mocha mugs and pewter saucers harmonize ideally with their mellow surroundings of thatch and stone and honeysuckle porch. This is as it should be for a cottage in the country is a phrase with magic in it still, as it was to late Georgian country-lovers over a century ago. But the magic is only more difficult to define than what is meant by cottage.

In this brief survey I have considered furnishings over a wide range of time and circumstance but with the emphasis strongly on what is still obtainable rather than on the exceptionally fine specimens that have found their way into museums. Old wills and inventories offer innumerable glimpses into homes of middling yeomen, tenant farmers, country craftsmen, small merchants, estate bailiffs and the like. Their furniture suggests the simple necessities shaped on traditional lines with little attempt to exploit passing vogues and this surely must be the basis for our choice of such furnishings today.

The cupboard or chair or long case clock lacks the elaboration of seaweed marquetry or carved cabochon that can declare the date of the city cabinet-maker's eye-catcher. Even the Britannia metal teapot has inherited notions from Sheffield plate to modify the extravagances of the silver-smith who first conceived the design. The transfer printed blue willow is as far from the porcelains that inspired it as the hand-coloured engraving from the original oil painting. But each has an air of honest value-for-money about it to appeal to the shrewd countryman and his equally hard-working wife and that appeal is timeless.

How much of the work was in fact country made is another matter. Many goods of one kind and another were hawked from door to door and others sold at markets, meeting comparable needs among country folk and their fellows in the provincial town. In any case they were close enough neighbours until the 19th-century sprawl of suburbia hardened and divided the images of town and country, just as changes in living standards hardened the division between labourer and gentlefolk, to the detriment of both.

It must be admitted, however, that the cottager like the cottage has tended to alter almost out of recognition down the years. Country village life in 18th-century England is now remote enough to appear a settled, peaceable existence. Yet even those who most deplore the appalling repercussions of the 19th century's industrial developments have to admit that the basic standard of living has gradually risen. That useful Swiss artist S. H. Grimm (working in England 1768-94) recorded unhappy glimpses of the common folk and their troubles and his delightful interior scenes are set not in cottages but in farmhouse kitchen and the like.

It is difficult now to visualise the 17th or 18th-century labourer's cottage without the golden light of the 19th century's desperate romanticism. Often enough the thatch was tattered, the mud inescapable and often too there was all the dust and dirt of some cottage industry shared among the whole family, such as cotton picking, or nail making, or skin curing. (A rabbit catcher, recorded by the Poulters' Company, possessed coney skins to the value of £187 8s. in 1677 when his home assets were no more than £2 4s.; another in 1700 had 1,250 skins in his keeping.) A small-holder in Co. Durham in 1631, with livestock worth £150 left his widow and six children a mere handful of household stuff valued at less than £4. A woman in the same county whose goods were thought worth inventory owned no more than a couple of chairs, a couple of beds, a table, a chest and a coffer, together with a kettle, a pot and a "crok upon the fyre".

Such records fail to do justice, however, to the simple but immensely pleasant surroundings of vast numbers of working folk whose long, hard days, spent mostly out of doors, were followed by comfortable evenings around the big fire of "hall" or farmhouse kitchen. Chickens might cluck sleepily among the rafters but the feather cushions eased the hard backs of the capacious saddle-seated chairs. The lamp might be dim and malodorous but firelight blazed on polished brass and copper. Their furnishings were seldom fashionable in the limited sense that diverted some rich folk with time on their hands and has tended too much to dominate the choice of subsequent collectors. Equally certainly they were seldom shoddy.

A blacksmith recorded in 1705 had an oval gateleg table and six rush chairs to set around it, three hanging cupboards as well as a dresser to display his pewter, a couch and a form for family and apprentice staff and probably, too, a considerable amount of built-in seating and cupboarding such as must have supplemented many a household's movables. In the 19th century the self-sufficing village with its farms and craftsmen gradually lost its identity and cheap factory products changed the whole pattern of its life but it would be foolish to generalize about the loss or gain to individuals.

The loss perhaps is to us today who regret especially the passing of the big, many-sided country household where the working farmer and his wife often shared not only work but their meals and scanty leisure with their staff; where only gradually the need was felt for a grandiose, stuffy little parlour genteelly furnished and draped against the on-slaughts of an increasingly noisy, dirty, workaday world outside. In 1825 William Cobbett complained that the countryman's old oak furniture, associated with plain manners and plentiful living, was falling into the decay of disuse. The farmhouse was becoming "too neat for a dirty-shoed carter to be allowed to come into". Worst of all, it had acquired a parlour furnished with mahogany, glass and the rest, "all as bare-faced upstart as any stock-jobber in the kingdom can boast of".

The country furnishings that appeal today could accept the carter, shoes and all, but also much that went into the farmhouse parlour. Today the collector's problem is to

15

decide how far to welcome the rich fare offered in the 19th century's attempts to come to terms with all the furnishing traditions of earlier generations. In furniture, for example, the romantic early 19th-century notions of Grecian, Medieval, Gothic and Elizabethan design all contributed to the rich plum cake of last century's baking. They are becoming less likely year by year to confuse today's more knowledgeable collectors but they were symptomatic of the wish to look backwards rather than thrusting ahead. J. C. Loudon, in his *Encyclopaedia of Cottage Farm and Villa Architecture and Furniture* 1833, considered "the principal Styles of Design in Furniture as at present executed in Britain" and accepted the Grecian as synonymous with "modern", considering it "by far the most prevalent". The Medievalist A. W. N. Pugin himself derided the application of Gothic ornament as fashionable disguise for modern furniture. Loudon referred to specific London firms with "extensive collections of Elizabethan and Dutch furniture and carvings from which a judicious compiler of exteriors might clothe skeleton frames, so as to produce objects of curiosity and interest, at a very trifling expense". Even C. L. Eastlake in his *Hints on Household Taste* 1868, suggested vaguely Elizabethan forms for his furniture, yet his intention was to get away from the heavy-handed elaborations of the mid-century years and he suggested, for example, oak and mahogany "stained black and covered with a thin varnish with hinges and escutcheons of white metal".

In previous centuries, traditional methods in design and construction had saved the wildest notions of ornament from interfering with sound craftsmanship. But now even when the Morris group produced honest furniture it proved mainly over-forceful and difficult to live with. Nevertheless, as Loudon noted in 1833, reaction was already creating a demand for a new kind of cottage furnishings. These were not the horrors of rustic work in cast iron but simple, serviceable pieces for the many who lived in the country from choice rather than by inherited privilege or disability. He illustrated and described such furnishings which he admitted "pretend to nothing more than what could be invented by any joiner who could read and draw and derive ideas from books".

It is for individual collectors to decide where to draw the line, how far to accept the transition from monotonous hand-labour to monotonous machine-minding, both taken for granted in their day. Some who accept cheap little Walton figures despise the Victorian flat-back. Some who love coloured stipple engravings abjure the Baxter print. Undoubtedly the 19th century's uninhibited delight in any and all possessions meant that its riches spilled plentifully into every kind of cottage dwelling, from copper lustre mugs to commemorative horse brasses. To return for a moment to furniture, as E. Gordon Roe has pointed out, mid-Victorian Wycombe could boast of making "a chair a minute all the year round—chairs that would not be unsightly in the handsomest sitting room, and which can be sold at 5s. each. More costly chairs are here produced, as well as the commonest rush-bottom chair of the old cottage pattern. But the light caned chair, stained to imitate rosewood or of the bright natural colour of the birch, and highly polished, finds a demand throughout the kingdom . . .".

Chapter One

R OUT CHAIR is a term to savour. It calls to mind the rampageous assemblies of the late 18th-century and Regency cartoonist, all noise and glitter, with these tough small chairs tossed around as weapons or flourished in acclamation while the myriad candles guttered and flared and the chandeliers tinkled vain protest. A rout was a term for any kind of party gathering but it also had a more ominous, violent meaning long before these cheap small chairs were first hired out in great numbers for entertaining in the grand manner. Sheraton defines them as "small painted chairs with rush bottoms".

Superb chairs from the 17th century onwards are to be found in mansion and museum and none more perfect in their distinctive ways than those of the early, middle and late 18th century. But these only emphasize the comfortless meagreness of the chairs almost invariably recorded in contemporaneous paintings and prints. Even through the comfort-loving 19th century the plain, tough style of the rout chair persisted for workaday use, for the garden, the beach, the bazaar, the concert hall. In comparison the chairs now regarded as the country cottagers' hard lot are often splendid pieces, functional like all good furniture, which meant satisfying the user's eye with a reasonable acknowledgment of passing fashion and his body with lasting ease.

Nowadays it is foolish to cast more than a glance at the ornate little Derbyshire-Yorkshire chairs apparently popular in the Midlands in the later 17th century, with backs conspicuously composed of arcaded balusters and knob finials or flat rails hooped and escalloped. But the 18th and 19th

19

centuries have left us a range of chairs more varied than may be imagined by some who seek only "fashion" styles and find themselves all too often acquiring merely the Victorians' near-copies of "Chippendale" and "Hepplewhite". These wooden country chairs include the splatback, the ladder-back and the spindle-back and its variant drunkard's chair, all with conventional construction; and the comb-back, hoop-back, smoker's bow, Mendlesham, scroll-back and plain kitchen "white Wycombe" that show an entirely different approach to the whole ancient matter of chair making. And if none offers the comfort of today's overstuffed easy chair it must be remembered that in the crowded cottage the bed was the major status symbol with its abundance of home-provided quilted and feather-filled furnishings. By the draught-hungry faggot fire only solid-backed settles could meet the needs of a sizeable family.

The splat-back chair of fashion offered new ideas of comfort and elegance by shaping the whole silhouette to fit the sitter's shoulders and spine. A cupid's bow cresting rail links the back verticals and the space between this cresting and the back seat rail is filled by a wood splat shaped in a shouldered vase profile. The country chair maker seldom attempted the "bended" back curved to fit the sitter but he soon accepted the conventions that projected the cresting in neat scrolls or ears beyond the back verticals and hand-pierced the splat in simple patterns.

The square-edged wooden seat riding over the seat rails may be plain and slippery but is more often surrounded by a low rim for a squab cushion. The legs are framed into the seat rails in the usual manner but are left plainly square except for chamfering on the inner corners and are linked on all four sides by plain stretchers. These are in thinner section than the legs but placed flush with their outer surfaces. More sophisticated chairs for hall and dining room often enough have similar legs but the surfaces are wave moulded and the stretchers usually in an *H* arrangement.

Sometimes a splat-back chair is found with a rush seat. This necessitated somewhat rounded seat rails meeting in square corners where the front legs are dowelled into them.

1. Country chairs with a long tradition of homely cottage service. The spindle-back (*upper left*) is one of several versions, the plain wooden seat fronted with a shaped apron and rimmed to hold a cushion. The elm wood ladder-back (*upper right*) has the characteristic waved cross rails and springy rush seat. The turned front legs are much simplified versions of the early 18th century's fashionable pad-footed cabriole and there is a typical swelling front stretcher. The low, extremely sturdy spindle-back (*lower left*) is often known as a drunkard's chair but was probably mainly a nursing chair. The saddle-seated rocker (*lower right*) is of elm and shows characteristic back and leg shaping of its period: this is dated to 1851.

2. Four Windsor chairs that show something of the range of design covered by this familiar term. *Upper left:* comb-back with ash "sticks" and legs driven into the elm seat. This probably dates to the third quarter of the 18th century. *Upper right:* comb-back windsor with central pierced splat strengthened by diagonal struts behind the back and with typical early leg shaping. Made in about the 1770s. *Lower left:* a late 18th-century example of the hoop-back with bent wood forming back and arm rails and cow's horn stretcher. The saddle rests somewhat uneasily on cabriole legs such as had been in fashion early in the century. *Lower right:* the comb-back in a simple mid-18th-century style showing the deep saddle shaping of the solid elm seat.

This, in fact, is a turner's chair, with little but the shapely cresting rail and splat in flat wood. Legs shaped by turning could be given slight knee and foot swelling as a gesture towards the more extravagant shaping of cabriole legs and pad feet. The slender stretchers are usually found in the turner's conventional arrangement of two at the back, two at each side, with a more massive stretcher decoratively turned across the front.

The turner was largely responsible, too, for the different parts of another favourite country chair, the spindle-back associated especially with Lancashire and the north. In this the cresting may ride over the verticals with the attractive eared outline found in the splat-back, or may be framed within the verticals like the cross rails below. An arm-chair may have three cross rails, three rows of spindles, but for single chairs two rows are more usual. Some enthusiasts claim that long thin spindles are to be associated with north Lancashire and the bolder spindles with the south of the county. A simple form of the chair with a single row of spindles and a plain wood seat is associated with Cumberland. Turned chairs suggesting bamboo were popular early and late in the 19th century in response to enthusiasm for Oriental notions. In these even the spindles may show bamboo swellings. Age may be judged to some extent by the curve of the front legs.

All these turner chairs show attractive details, expecially in the shapely profiles of their ornamental spindles. Even the tops of the back verticals and the tops of the front legs rising above the seat are finished in neat points—a turner's convention remembered in late Victorian chairs by Morris & Co.

The spindles tend to be grouped to the centre of the chair, offering much the same support as a splat. The plain-turned cross rails are scarcely thicker than the spindle ends but swell slightly where drilled for the spindles to be inserted. The legs tend to be broad at the knee, then deeply incised before tapering to feet in various bun shapes that would give long wear on damp stone floors without becoming unsightly. Sometimes there is a plain front stretcher as well as a higher one ornamentally turned.

Randle Holme in the 17th century illustrated a chair with spindles between seat and stretcher.

The north country's so-called drunkard's chair is a spindle-back variant made by the joiner, with only the rows of spindles supplied by the turner. This is very low and wide with a cresting rail often decoratively pierced above the row or two of spindles. The arms are wide, the feet often show slightly projecting toes and at the sides additional ground-level stretchers all help to make this an exceptionally steady chair but more in demand by the mother of young children, perhaps, than by the men of the family.

Many of the attractive features of the rush seated spindle-back chair were brought to the notice of a new class of customer in the second half of the 19th century by the firm of Morris & Co., established 1861. The period's aesthetes delighted in them, of course, but they were sought out, too, by many town and suburb dwellers with an inborn appreciation of plain country styles. Arm-chairs may be found and an occasional settee. These have short orna-mental spindles between top and cross rails and two lower cross rails often enclosing turned balls in the Mendlesham manner. Below, the slightly outflared tapering legs are linked by thin stretchers, two at the front and each side and one at the back. All the turning of verticals is entirely plain but the slanting supports of the arms are noticeable, passing through the sides of the seat to project for several inches below. A settee of the Morris type could be bought at the time for thirty-five shillings; an arm-chair for under ten shillings, "perhaps somewhat rough in the make".

The ladder-back, too, may be composed mainly of turned members. But its considerable charm lies in its three, four or five horizontal cross rails down its back. The arms, when there are any, rest on decorative extensions of the turned front legs and are set high above the rush seat to allow for a substantial feather cushion, with cross rails between arm and seat to keep it in place. Here again the turned legs may be straight, or show conventionalized modification of the cabriole knee and bun foot. There are usually two thin stretchers each side and sometimes in an

18th-century specimen two close-set at the front. Stubbs's Manufactory, offering "all Sorts of Yew Tree, Gothic and Windsor Chairs, Alcoves, and rural Seats, Garden Machines, Dyed Chairs, etc." on a trade card of 1790–1803—all illustrated—shows a ladder-back as the dyed chair, with rush seat and two front stretchers. The frequent alternative for the cottager was to have furniture "in the white"—unstained—and keep it clean with sand. (The "garden machine" was an invalid chair: Lockⁿ Foulger in the 1770s illustrated a simple comb-back windsor chair mounted on small wheels with a steering handle at the front in the style of the old bath chair.)

The ladder rails may be found in a range of outlines. In the best designs they decrease in width a little from the top to the lowest and each rail has at least three changes of curve. Sometimes attractive wave shaping is found, sometimes a simple cyma line. In the early 19th century many were made with the upper edge of each rail curving upwards towards the centre while the lower edge is straight where previously both were curved.

The country chairs still to be considered are very different from each other but all differ again from the conventional constructions so far described. In these the basic unit has been the pair of back vertical rails. The rail from cresting to floor is a single piece of wood curving a little to ensure the stability of a backward splay. Cresting and cross rails, seat and back stretchers all link these vertical members. In the windsor type, however, the unifying factor is the seat and this in itself was designed according to a different convention. The early splat-back has its seat rim for a cushion, the spindle- and ladder-backs have the spring of rush seating; the windsor type, with the back set at an angle for comfortable lounging, keeps the sitter from slipping off by hollowing out the seat a little and raising the centre of the expansive front and also the front corners so that the whole seat looks somewhat heart-shaped.

This saddle seat is nearly always found in pleasantly round-grained elm, ever the countryman's favourite seatwood. It has to be an extremely substantial block for on the upper face it must house the vertical members of back

23

and arms and on the under face the four widely splayed legs. This notion of wedging turned legs into a solid vertical wooden seat is as old as the three-legged milking stool. But the windsor was the earliest style of chair to show bent wood as a basis of contruction.

No one knows when or why the name originated but references have been found to japanned windsor chairs in the Duke of Chandos's library at Cannons in 1725 and mahogany specimens for St. James's Palace library about 1730. Windsor garden chairs were advertised in 1727 "painted green or in the wood" suggesting that already they were in demand for informal comfort indoors and out. They appear in many a Devis country garden conversation group. Apart from a minority they were essentially cheap. They were produced by primitive woodsman methods of spindle and dowel joints that could be shaped wherever a "bodger" set up his pole lathe in a woodland clearing. Beech and elm were abundantly available in the Buckinghamshire woods and the craft came to be associated with the region of Chepping Wycombe, now High Wycombe, where much of the woodland was owned by the Windsor family. But it was soon being made in the West Country, known merely as the stickback chair, and in the Midlands. In the early 19th century a heavy variety with particularly decorative splat and splendidly turned legs and arm supports came to be associated with Lancashire.

The windsor may be regarded as the first article of furniture to be mass produced, the various parts being prepared in the woods in quantity for speedy assembly. At its simplest, probably from at least as early as 1720, the back was composed merely of a row of plain-turned spindles or sticks dowelled into the seat and topped by a shaped cresting rail. This was the comb-back. Bent wood was first introduced to link the spindles midway up the back and curve round in the U shape of the seat so as to serve as arms. The back spindles passed through this and more spindles of half height supported the arm ends.

Apart from a few early free-legged specimens in the stool tradition it is usual to find stretchers controlling the outjutting legs. These are in the H arrangement familiar on most 18th-century chairs, and indeed some of these chairs have considerable pretensions to elegance. In this comb-back variety the cresting is in curved, scrolling outline, usually with pronounced ears, and the stick spindles may flank a central flat splat rising from a solid "shoe" attached to the back of the seat. In a fine quality chair, such as those in very early mahogany made for St. James's, the early spoke leg turning may have been permissible for the back legs, but at the front a full-kneed cabriole outline on a pad foot would be expected, requiring much more wood and looking slightly rakish when combined with the windsor's up-cornered saddle seat.

From the 1760s a few makers were turning out extremely handsome windsors in yew wood in so-called Gothic style. In this design three back splats and two arm supports are pierced in church-window patterns. It seems that Gothic garden chairs continued to be made into the 19th century, long after the leisurely well-to-do had abandoned their romantic notion of quaint little "Gothic cells" of shell work and other amateur elegance popular in the 1760s.

The majority of this breed, however, were country chairs for farmhouse and prosperous cottage. The comb-back with shaped cresting supported by plain turned sticks was augmented by the comb-back with a central splat. The splayed legs were linked by turned stretchers, the side ones swelling a little to receive a cross stretcher usually turned with a pattern of swells. For greater strength the back might be braced with a pair of struts slanting down to a narrow bob-tail jutting out from the back edge of the seat and this is noted occasionally, too, on the low-back variety of hoop-back.

Comb-backs continued to be advertised until late in the 18th century but by the mid-century, it appears, the chair maker had discovered that a hoop of wood such as formed the arms could be used instead of shaped cresting and would result in a chair that would bounce rather than disintegrate when carelessly handled on stone flagged floors. The hooped bar in rectangular section may rise either from the arms—the high-back type—or from the back corners of the seat—the low-back—to enclose the sticks and also, if required, a central splat. Shorter curves support the arm ends and often the stretcher arrangement is modified to what is sometimes called the cow's horn or crinoline line. This has a backward curved hoop linking the front legs and short straight stretchers spurring off from this to the back legs.

All this bent work is of springy, close-grained yew, steamed with only part of the bark removed, then levered into shape and cooled in a clamp. And all the ends were secured by dowelling into the seat. The spindle ends were heated before being driven into hoop and seat wood so that as they cooled and expanded they fitted extremely tightly. Several other native woods may be found in the one chair—elm for the seat, straight-grained beech or, more rarely, ash or chestnut for the legs. But the heavy Lancashire windsor is often of tawny yew wood throughout.

It is thought that the earliest comb-back windsors of about the 1720s with plain stick backs had the plain spoke type of leg. In this design the main swelling is about two-thirds of the way from the top, with below this a ball knop and finally a substantial plain foot, almost a hoof. Then came modified cabriole legs in the wake of fashion, noted on some of the earliest hoop-backs. Thereafter a slightly different style of leg turning was used, continued into Victorian days. This somewhat suggests the early leg in reverse with the ball knop a little below the seat and a downward taper. There is no more than a minor swelling at ankle height though this ankle was more pronounced, as on all chairs, in Victorian days. The purpose of the swell was to accommodate the side stretchers, or the curving cow's horn. The presence of a splat is no indication of early manufacture but the perforated splat motifs of wheel and Prince of Wales feathers date only from about 1790 onwards.

The old comb-back often has a dip in the centre of the cresting to rest a sleepy head; the hoop back is inhospitable, requiring tall cushions—long cushions to the collector of old embroideries—to ease the sitter's rest. For a more comfortable back support, but with no risk at all of slumber, the turn of the 18th–19th centuries produced what is sometimes known as the smoker's bow, with the same construction of seat and legs but with a few substantial spindles, decoratively turned, supporting wide flat arms that curve deeply round the sitter. The back cresting, several inches deep, rises directly from the arm rest so that, above the seat, the chair is reminiscent of the serviceable little corner chair of the mid-Georgian's study or library. In the Victorian version the scroll of the hand-rests turns downward instead of outward and the chair has lost its jaunty air.

The Suffolk variant of the windsor is the Mendlesham, the back composed of narrow splats between cresting and cross rails. Often both these rails are in duplicate, housing small balls; the arm supports are curved, not bent, but the saddle seat and dowelled legs preserve the windsor tradition. This was a chair of the late 18th and early 19th centuries and, like the smoker's bow, contributed to the general acceptance of the 19th century's endlessly popular kitchen chair, still taken as a matter of course through much of the present century.

This probably was the kind J. C. Loudon meant in his *Cottage Furniture* when he dismissed the windsor with the single comment that it was one of the best kitchen chairs in general use in the Midland counties. Here, still, is the same style of seat and leg, but this is a space-saving single chair and the back is topped by a wide cresting, slightly crescent-shaped and at best finished with a small scroll silhouette at each end. This rides over the back support which is found in a number of styles. There may be a row of ornamental baluster spindles or a couple of spindles flanking a splat or, as a third alternative, a row of spindles plainly stick turned with no more than a slight central swelling. Sometimes there is a pair of shaped side rails curving forward a little and broadening at the seat junction: with a wide cresting these may enclose a row of plain turned spindles or slightly back-fitting laths of rectangular section. By as early as the 1830s, however, such verticals might enclose no better than a plain top rail and a plain cross rail. The cross rail at its best is the one small effort at ornament, then, with a central scrolled-over support for the small of the sitter's back.

A curious rarity is the double windsor, suggesting a

27

couple of comb-backs with splats and spindles, but with the double cresting as a single entity and an arm cross rail following the outline of the two-saddle seat. An extra leg supports the front. This would allow two people to sit in comfort by the fire but would not offer the draught-free cosiness, the sense of a room within a room, that could be created with a high-backed settle.

The settle as a chest with solid high back and arms was familiar in medieval days, but any found today are unlikely to date earlier than the 18th century. These have high panelled backs but the scrolling arms are open, long retaining the solid, nearly flat curves of the early panelled chair. These arms rest upon extensions of the corner stiles of the framed-up chest portion below: they are flush with the uprights on the outer sides but on the inner sides considerable tapering is required to make a neat union as the arms' scrolling ends are comparatively narrow. This detail may be observed, too, in settles of the 17th and 18th centuries when the arms rest upon extensions of the front legs. These later settles make extremely pleasant furnishings. Usually there are central legs at front and back, and front and back stretchers: occasionally the cresting and front stretcher may be carved. More usually the simple panelling is rimmed with slightly projecting moulding and the only ornament is the brief knop turning on the arm rests and front legs between the substantial blocks left for jointing. The style of the panelling can be compared with work on wall and chest furniture as some guide to dating, allowing, as ever, for the time lag while the country furniture maker absorbed each change of fashion.

A detail sometimes removed from an old settle is the series of holes in the seat rails intended for the criss-cross of ropes that support the cushion seat. Replacement rails, even when correctly bored, often lack the channels between the holes that made the ropes fit neatly. It may be mentioned that settees with panelled backs and plain wooden seating were often used as hall furniture in a large house, being suited for the outdoor clothing of waiting messengers, sedan chair men and the like. But these lack the settle's air of expansive comfort. As Randle Holme defined the piece in the 17th

3. The most ornate style of the essentially welcoming, comfortable windsor chair. *Above:* two so-called "Gothic" windsors. Specimens of this style and quality are a delight in every detail, from the "church window" carving to the upcurving line where the saddle seat meets the modified cabriole leg. *Below left:* a so-called Lancashire windsor of the early 19th century. These are usually found in resilient yew wood throughout. The splats are shaped and pierced, the arms wide, with scrolling hand rests and supported on spindles as elaborately turned as the substantial legs and cross stretcher. *Below right:* a particularly endearing little chair sturdily constructed for a child, the springy framework in bent yew wood being especially suitable for children's furniture. This is 2 feet tall.

4. Two dressers in the style that preceded the tall shelved and canopied piece and that was long retained as a pleasant alternative, sometimes with hanging shelves on the wall above. The upper specimen is in the bold style of the later 17th century, the three drawers enriched with deep mouldings mitred at every corner and the front legs turned in baluster shapes. An interesting detail is the low rim around the top, to keep vessels from sliding off its well-polished surface. The later specimen below shows detail more usual on walnut or mahogany than oak. The elaborately pierced apron links exceptionally shapely legs with the shell knee-carving and ball-and-claw foot introduced as an early Georgian fashion.

century it was so called because of its massive weight so that of necessity it "still abideth in its own station".

The ultimate in settles as country furniture, perhaps, might be considered to be the garden seat. These hard, straight-backed rustic settees have such a Victorian air to them that it is surprising, perhaps, to find them illustrated, for example, in the 1773 trade card of Lock[n] Foulger "at Wallam Green" and almost exactly repeated by Stubbs's Manufactory at the century's end. Foulger shows one with its ram-rod back pierced in Gothic church window ornament, a style that was popular for a time in establishments serving light refreshments. His alternative suggestion is a seat entirely composed of rustic branches, knobbly enough to drive any drowsy gardeners back to their tasks.

Chapter Two

———————

PLATES, dishes and platters, saucers for spicy dressings, bowls for soups and spoonmeats—twelve of everything in gleaming, hard-scoured pewter made a splendid array under the fine old name of a garnish. By the 18th century every sizeable farmhouse kitchen and prosperous cottage had such treasure paraded in full splendour upon the open shelves or racks over the dresser. By setting the plates with their bases turned outwards the proud housewife could display their brightness unmarred by knife scratches and preserved their working surfaces from the inevitable dust of busy room and open hearth. Later collectors have found these old dresser racks superb settings for their china table wares. But they seldom realize perhaps, that the dresser as we know it today first came into use no earlier than the end of the 17th century.

Here it may be well to sort out the various pieces of furniture associated in this way with a parade of possessions. In the early home, rich or not so rich, the bed furnishings were second only to the funeral arrangements as a declaration of status, and next to the bed the display of gold and silver plate or their tinny substitutes at table. In a rich establishment the table was augmented by tiered shelving at the side for the handsome cups and tankards brought into use for freshly poured drinks in the course of a meal. Even a lesser home would have its side table—its cup-board. This was the early dresser, a simple table, long and narrow for easy access and often fitted with a row of drawers in the apron for locking away the owner's few valuable pieces, such as christening spoons.

The grandeur of the court and mansion cupboard may

be traced in the early court cupboard, sometimes now called a buffet. Instead of a single long table top this has two or three tiers of open shelving on massive cup-and-cover supports: it passed out of fashion along with this type of pillar. There are arguments both ways as to whether the word court has any bearing on its status. On the Continent the owner's rank long determined the number of tiers of plate he might put on show. But the word, meaning short in French, might indicate merely that this was a shortened version of the long side table, tiered to take less space in a crowded room. Randle Holme (1627–99) includes "side tables or court cubberts" for the cups, sugar box and the like in the dining room. In a typical late Elizabethan inventory Thomas Brickwell, captain of the garrison at Berwick, had two court cupboards and a great cupboard in his hall and another court cupboard in his great chamber, but for storage here he had seven chests, a trunk and a little coffer.

This word cup-board in the early sense of a board or table is found too in the livery cupboard where the kitchen staff set out, or delivered, small items such as food and candles for members of the household to take to their rooms. Early corner cupboards are to be noted too, composed of tiers of open shelving. Cupboarding in the modern sense of the word was covered by such phrases as a "cupboard with aumbries" or more simply by the comprehensive word press, the most splendid of these being what we know now as the hall or parlour cupboard and the Welsh near-relatives of deudarn and tridarn (Chapter Three).

Seventeenth-century dressers remain in the form of long side tables often with drawers in the apron. Two dressers of wainscot (Baltic imported oak) with setwork (inlay) were valued at 40s. in the 1596 inventory of Robert Atkynson, former Sheriff of Newcastle. Such a table in oak or fruitwood would serve the merchant or yeoman farmer although more often than not it must have displayed more tinware or coarse eathernware than silver plate. Many reproductions were made in the 1920s. Probably not until about 1690 was the table given a low backboard with a moulded top. This might prop up the plates on show but sometimes included small drawers now inevitably known as spice drawers, reflecting a general furniture fashion of the period. The notion soon passed for the dresser was essentially a country furniture joiner's job in wainscot oak or cheaper local wood and lost touch with the fashion world where tables termed sideboards eventually took shape as the furniture we know by that name today.

Meantime the prospering farmer acquired a liking for the gaily decorated platters of painted English delft and pictorial slip ware that may be regarded too as substitute wares, supplied for the less wealthy wishing to imitate costly displays of Chinese porcelains. For the dresser this meant a plate rack hung above it, usually with three shelves and a projecting canopy fastened to the wall by iron staples. Thereupon this arrangement of plate rack and table became a single unit under the name of dresser. Narrow safety rails were fitted to the shelves top and bottom in early racks but on these the backboards appear usually to be later additions. The plate rack alone may be found too, occasionally with a bar across the centre of each shelf space so that the plates can lean outwards in safety, acquiring less dust and reflecting light to the lower regions of the room.

Such high dressers had been in use for a long time on the Continent. But the style of their treatment, allowing for the time lag between cabinet maker and country joiner, shows that the English—and Welsh—examples found today are mainly Georgian.

It is intriguing to observe the small details of fashion worked into many of these dressers which are immensely handsome pieces of furniture. The canopy over the shelves may be shaped in variously curved patterns such as opposing scrolls and in the second half of the 18th century was often pierced. The shelves are supported on side uprights in moulded profile and occasionally in the centre by turned spindles. Sometimes the canopy corners end in short pendant knobs, a detail copied from hall or parlour cupboards where they may be found as vestiges of the bulbous pillars supporting the upper structure in the 16th–17th centuries.

Sometimes too there is a small concession to the 18th

5. Such a fine specimen explains why pride of place was given to the oak dresser in innumerable 18th-century homes. This example shows the design at its most splendid with bold cornice and ornamental frieze. The shelves are supported on decoratively shaped side verticals, small shelf rims securing the array of plates that would reflect light and colour into the room. Below, the drawers and cupboards are fronted with the fielded panels of 18th-century work in solid oak which long retained the framed-up mortise-and-tenon method of construction.

6. Small plainly constructed dresser of solid oak. Viewed from the end, it is easy to see how the early side-board for preparing and serving food was transformed into a capacious cupboarded piece with drawers and doors to house table ware and tools below. Then, when still more shelf space was required, a yet more elaborate piece might be evolved by adding a superstructure with shelves and backboard topped by a canopy supported on corner pillars to keep dust from the pictorial platters—in slipware, perhaps, or Staffordshire blue—long known by their homely name of rack plates.

century's liking for bland-faced veneers. In the oak dresser there was no way of concealing the meeting of each shelf end with the supporting upright but the line may be masked and the sense of cohesion increased by double rows of gouge-cuts along the edges, with the inner row following the angle of the join and running along the shelf edge.

Below the table top the row of three or four drawers carry expansive loop handles and in early work the keyhole escutcheons are in similar wide-eared outline; more waved moulding and occasional piercing ornaments the apron below and in high quality work the front legs are frequently in modified cabriole outline, including a central leg at the front making a conspicuous feature of its shell carving on the knee. Very occasionally the legs end in richly carved claw-and-ball feet.

This general design is found with many minor variants and it is rash to attribute all dressers to North Wales if the drawers in the apron have cupboards below or to Yorkshire if there is a clock in the framing. In any case the clock, by its construction, usually appears to be a 19th-century feature and the term Welsh dresser is late Victorian.

The most obvious development was the introduction of a pot board linking the legs a little above the ground. This may rest on substantial bracket feet in the swelling cabriole profile at the front, with three or four turned spindles linking the board with the apron framing of the drawers above. But by fully enclosing the lower portion the joiner made a more practical piece of furniture. In a good specimen the cupboard doors are extremely attractive. These may flank a central section in the same fielded panel contruction, rounded arches to the panel tops being followed by ogee outlines. As an important detail, noted also when long case clocks entered workaday farmhouse and villa, the flooring is lifted well clear of the ground by simple brackets—later plainly turned feet.

Sometimes cupboards were introduced in the upper section too and these might well justify the spice cupboard reputation. Usually these flank the lower shelves, leaving a wide shelf at the top for expansive pictorial "rack plates." Again the arched shaping of the fielded panels is often delightful. Sometimes there is considerable resemblance to the style of long case clock body work, as could be expected of craftsmen with the same class of market in view. Even the pair of arching rose-topped scrolls—the broken swan-neck pediment—typical of innumerable later 18th-century clock hoods may be found as cresting to the dresser's small spice cupboards of the same period.

In the same tradition in a late dresser the side supports to the shelving may be concealed by wide reeded columns. In the same way, too, as on other country furniture, the dresser may show veneered detail such as cross banded borders of mahogany, never a very happy combination with oak, and small inlay motifs such as shells and curling leaves and many-petalled flowers bought as complete units from specialist marquetry men to ornament the small cupboard doors. An attractive edging around these doors and also sometimes on the drawers is a band of black and white inlay either as checker stringing or as herringbone pattern in light and dark woods.

This kind of detail, like the wavy frieze edging each shelf, was a late attempt to dress up what was, perhaps, beginning to lose its self-assurance. By 1833 Loudon in his Encyclopaedia noted the dresser as a fixture, probably having in mind the plain factory-made type resting at the back upon a fillet attached to the wall instead of standing free. Such a piece, he asserted, was "essential to every kitchen, but more especially to that of the cottage to whom they serve both as dressers and sideboards".

The corner cupboard, as I mentioned above, had its beginning in William III's reign as another piece of open display furniture. An occasional specimen remains from the early 18th century built originally into a corner as a permanent group of open shelves. This was transformed into an extremely ornamental structure when it was topped by the porch effect or a half-dome sometimes rayed with applied ribs or carved in the shape of a shell and supported by half hidden pilasters. More reeded pilasters might then flank the opening, under an outer arch of carved moulding that framed the top. With such attractive detail this was essentially a piece for the well-to-do home, designed to fit in with

34

surrounding panelling. Every detail was carefully finished, the shelves edged in attractive curves and the whole interior richly coloured, most often a pleasant tone of deep sky blue but sometimes red, green or yellow, with the shell above picked out in gilding.

Below table level it was usual to introduce a simple cupboard door and the piece soon tended to lose its early character by becoming wholly enclosed, as cupboarding in the modern sense, with two doors for the upper section and one below. The upper doors were shaped in the familiar Queen Anne style of rounded arch in high-quality work but might be square at the top, merely with arching panels, on simple provincial work. Such a piece is of interest here because its usefulness in a crowded room prompted the development of less lofty, free-standing corner cupboards. These were being made in Wales by the beginning of the 18th century but among collectors they have tended to be overshadowed by the now extremely popular hanging corner cupboard.

In the simple country specimen more than a hint of the contemporaneous dresser may be noted. Admittedly glazing was introduced on fashionable drawing room examples in the 1740s and eventually found its way on to more workaday pieces suited to the farmhouse parlour. But it is far more usual to find all doors panelled, the plain oak or fruitwood possibly given mouldings in a contrasting wood. In its later phases it much resembled the hanging version but the collector may welcome its more substantial sturdiness and recognize the fact that it long retained its usefulness, sometimes with the lower cupboarding replaced by three drawers. Loudon in 1833 illustrates a built-in four-door specimen, the upper doors glazed but without the ornament of glazing bars to hide the straight shelving.

Chapter Three

CHESTS AND CUPBOARDS

PEWTER or pottery could decorate the plainest farm-house or cottage dresser but the furniture for storing household goods depended entirely on the maker's sense of design and the length of his client's stocking purse. Labour in the 17th and 18th centuries was cheap; crafts-manship implied certain standards in the simpler basic skills, but good materials were always costly. The occasional inventory of a small Elizabethan or Stuart home usually includes a chest or two, but it is not always easy now to define the furniture that was most usually meant by such names as press, hutch, ark, aumbry and the like.

Chests are so familiar and so widely illustrated that prob-ably there is little need to go through the detail of their evolution. At Anne of Cleves House, Lewes, there is a fine salting tub of the 1400s dug out of a massive log. The developments from log to pegged and boarded chests and the niceties of framed-up panelled construction are mainly of historical interest: the styles of panelling and carving and the details of hinge and lock have been reproduced with such devastating thoroughness that now every carved inscription, every incised date, is deeply suspect.

Collectors today choose for sound framing, rich surface patina and a general air of unpretentiousness. They know they are unlikely to find specimens in working condition that date earlier than the late 17th century and these only in a style that was so unobtrusively useful that it continued popular generation after generation for locking away blankets, clothing, books and most especially great quanti-ties of linen sheets and napery. This linen was handed down in many a family—sometimes even in those whose movable

36

furniture consisted of little worth recording save the chests to keep it in. As a concession to tidiness there is often a small tray or till attached near the top of the chest at one end but the furniture's convenience lies in the fact that a single lock secures it against all normal hazards and it serves as table and chair when need arises. Randle Holme (1627–99) distinguishes a chest from a coffer by this "want of a circular lid".

The most usual type is plainly framed up with ornamentally moulded corner stiles housing the cross rails and central vertical muntin that together surround the loosely held panels, allowing the oak to respond to atmospheric changes. The mouldings around the panels retain the stone-mason's splay at the botton. Carved ornament is usually restricted to simple lunette or guilloche patterns in low relief along the upper cross rail below the lid, with perhaps a formal lozenge in the centre of each front panel. End panels are plain.

The lid surface may show traces of the dowel pins that secure the bearers on its underside: these rest outside the ends of the chest body when the lid is closed and ensure a firm fit as well as strengthening the lid. The wood of the lid may also show slight protuberances near the back where simple staple hinges have been fixed inside. But often in a chest of good quality the lid too consists of framed panels with an edge of plain thumb moulding. There may be an expansive lock escutcheon fitting a hinged hasp on the lid but such detail is often missing or anachronistically replaced. Even such a simple chest ought to prove extremely substantial when opened. Anything flimsy should be suspect at once.

The most substantial of all, also introduced in the 17th century, has less satisfactory ornament, this being applied instead of forming an integral part of the construction. This appeared at a time when English workmen were attempting to absorb many Continental ideas but it is essentially heavy country work, stubbornly refusing to suggest high fashion. Some of this ornament may be in willow wood dyed to suggest ebony, including split turnings, bosses and projecting panels. Sometimes heavy mouldings are squared up with mitred corners in elaborate outlines to suggest panelling. Understandably this style of chest furniture soon produced a reaction and high fashion turned with relief to flat, construction-effacing veneers.

As a step towards the chest of drawers such a chest may have two or three drawers under the main framework—bottom drawers of the bride-to-be—often separated by a strip of applied moulding above the heavily moulded base. Sometimes as a final absurdity the corner stiles are extended as feet below this moulding but as often there are pleasantly substantial bun feet.

The other style of chest dating from the 17th century onwards that occasionally turns up is the travelling trunk (and the efforts to make strong yet portable luggage offer many intriguing pieces for the collector, not least attractive the 18th century's occasional horsehair trunk with leather strappings). These were Randle Holme's coffers, with slightly domed lids to throw off the rain. The finest were weather-proofed with leather and this was protected from the rub of wear by close nailing in attractive patterns. This was the work of the cofferer. I have noticed the term London chest applied to one in 1598. Such details as the heavy metal corner strappings may be extremely handsome but allusions to royalty in the nail patterns must be taken as indicating an original association with some ministry or government department rather than direct service to the monarch.

Drawers secured by locks may be included under the main chest but were no more than a concession to a fashion for more specialized furnishings: cabinet makers produced chests of drawers for every phase of fashion through the 18th century but they never wholly ousted the country joiner's plain chest-of-all-work. Nowadays it is usual to regard 18th-century versions as blanket chests. Some produced early in the century are extremely plain in shape with rounded lid, straight sides and short bracket feet, a style that lent itself to amateur japanned ornament in imitation of rich Oriental lacquer. The domed lid associated with the period's liking for rounded curves protected the fleeting ornament from the rub of table top use but nevertheless these now tend to have a mellow, faded look that would not be out of place in a cottage bedroom.

The most attractive early 18th-century chests, perhaps, are those with plain flat lids, thumb moulded at the edge, and framed panels at the front in the simplest fielded style. Below the chest there may be a couple of drawers and below these again a shapely scrolling apron curving down to squat little legs in bowed cabriole outline. Such a chest in oak or native fruitwood is a delightful country adaptation of the handsome plain mahogany chest or chest-and-drawers often called a mule chest on a separate cabriole-legged stand. Sometimes the drawers are in the stand instead so that the chest is less ponderous to lift by its handsome end handles. But for farmhouse and cottage use the plain chest on short straight legs was the classic favourite.

For hanging clothes and general purpose storage, a well-equipped home would have at least one massive cupboard, often a built-in fixture. A clothes cupboard with deep shelves was probably the kind of furniture most usually meant in references to a press in early inventories—a piece for sleeping apartments and general purpose rooms but essentially a simple structure. By the 17th century such a cupboard might combine a couple of drawers in the frieze with a deep double-doored cupboard below in a straight-forward framed-up style. The panelling suggests some indication of the date though this is a simple traditional piece. The really decorative cupboard of early days was the piece now known as a hall or parlour cupboard: a parlour was defined in the 18th century as a ground-floor room for the entertainment of company. For a time collectors applied the term court cupboard to such a piece, but mistakenly it seems: I consider this point in Chapter Two. In the very early days these hall cupboards were for the lord of the manor but eventually fashion passed on, leaving the country furniture maker to continue his modified versions of the piece which are among the finest furnishings associated with prospering farmhouse and country homestead.

The story of the parlour cupboard began when Elizabethan furniture joiners transformed a plain double cupboard into a shoulder-high decorative piece by adding an upper structure. This consisted of two small cupboards flanking a central panel for secret storage, all set back from the edge of the cupboard top so that this formed a narrow shelf. Above the small cupboards a high cornice extended to the full depth of the lower cupboards and was supported at the front by a couple of pillars resting on the corners of the shelf.

This furniture was thus a double modification of what is now regarded as the court cup-board or three-tiered side table. The upper tiers retained the two bulbous pillar supports but behind them introduced the small cupboards: specimens are to be found with only this upper section modified in this way. But for the most ornate hall or parlour cupboard the lower tier was entirely filled in with doors and panels. In the late 16th and 17th centuries the piece was lavishly carved and often decorated with inlays but as the 17th century progressed the tendency was towards less flamboyant ornament, with low relief carving in simple repetitive patterns on the cornice frieze and the upper cupboarding. Even the massive pillars were reduced to baluster shapes until replaced by short turned pendant bosses.

Like the chest the parlour cupboard passed through a phase of glued-on ornament, such as projecting mouldings with carefully elaborate mitred corners and spindle shapes turned and split lengthwise. Geometrical inlay was in keeping with this style, in contrasting woods, bone and mother-of-pearl. But even by the late years of the 17th century the piece was out of fashion, with no more than minor low relief carving on the upper stage and wide cupboard doors below bearing the characteristic panelling composed of a horizontal panel above two vertical panels for each door. Some of these early 18th-century cupboards have the greatest attraction of all, with fielded panels to upper and lower cupboard doors. Often there is a row of drawers in the frieze and another above the lower cupboarding, below what was now only a narrow shelf as the upper cupboards grew deeper and only terminal pendant knobs remained from the early pillars.

From late in the 17th century the Welsh had a liking for the two-stage cupboard known as the cwpwrdd deuddarn and also for their more distinctive form of cwpwrdd tridarn, a three-stage cupboard with the topmost portion a hooded canopy supported on balusters at the sides. This served for display like a deep dresser shelf. Welsh cupboards were made throughout the 18th century and the two-stage version might be given a canopy to increase its value at a more recent date. It is well to realize also that imitations of hall or parlour cupboards in nearly, but never quite, all their Elizabethan magnificence were the delight of many romantic early Victorians. These were stained black instead of showing the hard-surfaced lustrous brown of antique oak.

Corner cupboards too are mainly of interest to those seeking cottage antiques when they date to the period of fashion's decline. But in this case their role was always a minor one, too insignificant for the attention of famous furniture designers. They were hung upon parlour or living room or kitchen walls by the simple means of drilling holes in the back boards and driving heavy wrought iron nails into the wall behind. They were made from the early years of the 18th century until far into the 19th but the majority were delightfully simple and may be found in a wide variety of woods including oak, walnut, mahogany, fruitwoods and japanned imitations of Oriental lacquer.

An occasional early specimen may date before the 18th century, but the majority found today are no earlier than the 1760s. The design varied comparatively little but comparison with other country furniture may indicate the approximate date. The cornice was obviously intended to be set above eye level and the cupboard's boarded top could be used for displaying a few treasures. In the wake of fashion there was some use of a hooded cornice, however, and the subsequent arching swan-neck broken pediment found on so much of the 18th century's pleasant provincial furniture.

The straight top may be emphasized by dentil or arcaded moulding. But there is comparatively little variation in size or shape, the average width being about 22 inches, height between 40 and 50 inches. There may be one door or two, most often plainly panelled, and usually hung on brass H hinges. But the country furniture maker seldom attempted the convex double doors of the cabinet maker. The cupboard's shape was much improved by the usual habit of flanking it with splayed corners so that it could be reasonably deep—usually about 16 inches—without excessive width. Some early specimens in oak extend flatly from wall to wall but later the design was modified to the splayed style that had proved successful in walnut and mahogany.

Inside, the shelves might have the attractively shaped edges of fashionable work and the whole effect was immensely enriched by the interior colouring, usually soft red or pale green but sometimes blue or yellow.

Other antique cupboards for miscellaneous purposes may be difficult to come by in good condition although many interesting versions of the ark or food hutch were made. These have ventilation holes arranged in decorative patterns often all over the vertical surfaces, the holes doubtless often covered originally on the inside with coarse haircloth to keep out flies, just as the bacon was wrapped to hang from the rafters. The sloping top is a frequent feature in early specimens. It is easy to understand its purpose in, for example, the north country "dresser" dated 1659 at the Victoria and Albert Museum. This offers only a single shelf for displaying table ware protected from dust by a pillar-supported canopy and probably intended to fit under a sloping roof. But it has a deep chest compartment below for storage. Here the slant of the lid ensures that it will always be accessible whereas a flat chest tended to be used as a table if not as a seat. The style of ventilated slanting lidded food hutch with projecting knob ornament on its front corner stiles is associated with the eastern counties and sometimes called a game cupboard.

For bacon the most attractive storage took shape in the 17th century as the high-backed settle. The doors of the tall shallow cupboards housing the sides of bacon form the back of the settle and there is usually additional chest storage space under the seat. At its most impressive such a settle cupboard has not only a moulded cornice but additional small cupboarding projecting above the sitters' heads. Wide flattish arms on turned supports make this a comfortable, homely piece for the fireside of a room that met most of its occupants' needs with dignity and unpretentious charm.

Chapter Four

———————

FAR from being occasional, the small tables in most homes today tend to be those in most frequent demand, able to be whisked away single-handed but never far out of sight. Obviously they are far older than the chance Elizabethan reference in will or inventory and usually it is impossible to give more than a rough dating. Here I can indicate the general trends of fashion so that collectors can see where a favourite specimen fits into the story. But the joy of such pieces is their obvious straightforward functionalism and their continuous production must be accepted as a background basis to the more fashionable and ephemeral styles concurrently evolved.

Knowledgeable collectors may be able to judge when wood is old and when the variations in tone and texture at the joints indicate that it has been serving its present purpose for many generations and is not merely old wood remade-up. Such details as hinges and drawer handles are usually most suspect when in very early style; but when in the natural course of use replacements have been introduced there is usually some sign of the earlier nail or screw holes— and even such holes have to be convincingly old.

The change from nails to screws is a useful date peg but later amateur repairers can often confuse the issue here. Hand-made screws for wood began to replace nails in the later 17th century and made it possible to hinge the thin flaps of the gateleg table from the underside, though often a slight undulation on the upper surface shows where each screw has been driven home. At this time the hinges were of wrought iron, with their holes not yet countersunk, so that nails or screw heads stood out slightly above the

44

surface. In the 18th century screws came to be used, too, to supplement glue for attaching the top to its framing; large screws driven in obliquely from beneath, as is still the way with these tables. The small early brass screws, hand filed, are very different from the later product cut on the lathe from about 1760; gimlet-pointed screws made by machine date only from about the middle of the 19th century.

To some extent, too, glue replaced the dowel pins for securing mortise and tenon joints, although the joints themselves remained the most satisfactory method of securing end grain to side grain and throughout the long success of gateleg tables evidence of their universal application is provided by the legs and stretchers turned and cut into a range of shapely patterns but invariably left in the square for every joint. This is found even in the spider gatelegs of the 1760s–70s, delicately turned in mahogany.

Hinges on some of the earliest folding tables were of wrought iron, those for the upward-folding flaps being rule hinges attached to the edges of the wood where nails would obtain adequate purchase. For the folding legs butterfly hinges could be used but the clever joiner obtained better and cheaper results with a pair of wood hinges for each movable leg, working on the table's underframing and stretcher. As a simple alternative the gateleg framing was soon made to pivot directly between the table underframing and the stretcher. Deep wooden hinges are characteristic of the 18th century's gate tables when part of the underframing moved with the leg.

When all this is said, however, it remain for collectors to choose for their own pleasure of eye and finger, for good design, mellowed surfaces, strong construction. Small tables for family dining, for placing under wall mirrors to hold candles, for games and writing and bedroom use, all have a long history. John Coote of Bury St. Edmunds willed his "best faldyn table" as early as 1502 and attractive specimens remain from the early 17th century. The open top is most often round. Closed into a semi-circle it fitted neatly against the wall, the top folding back upon itself to rest upon the semi-circular fixed framing mounted on three fixed legs with framing of similar shape or a solid base-board a few inches above the floor. To support the open flap an extra leg or a half leg, divided vertically from one of the fixed rear legs, swung out, being hinged to the centre of the straight back framing and back stretcher.

Sometimes the fixed top of the table could also be opened on a further pair of hinges, allowing access to a shallow well for storage, a lock and key providing the least conspicuous form of fastening, which had to be secure when the table was lifted. This was then to its Stuart user a pair of writing tables, using the term in a sense we have almost forgotten: the set-out for backgammon would scarcely be recognized today by its once-usual "pair of tables", nor a necklace as a pair of beads, though the pair of steps remains.

At the Victoria and Albert Museum a tiny table, dated 1625–50, has six sides when open, but the three small triangular flaps all fold in on themselves to make a triangular top: here the hinges are necessarily of the more conspicuous butterfly type which, with no more than brass pins to secure them, would limit the table's size. The triangular leg arrangement with a fourth leg in the centre is familiar on many an early cottage table with a round top.

These early folding tables are interesting but their direct successors were the writing and card tables of the 18th century which tend to be the exquisites of the mansion worked out in walnut and mahogany. Six-sided and eight-sided folding tables were frequent alternatives to the circle, but when the top was rectangular, opening to a square, the flap required two legs to be steady enough for writing or gaming. Here the hinged leg work was restricted to one side and this could be turned to the wall: when closed the piece was then a handsome little side table.

The development for more everyday use and especially at first for family dining in the privacy of the parlour was the falling table, with flaps that hung down instead of folding back, and the earliest of these was the gateleg. This gave place to the gate table in fashionable homes as soon as vastly tough mahogany made it possible to load the weight of a massive meal upon a rectangular table top supported merely by four legs—without stretchers—one under the middle of each side. The less fettered design made for the

46

diners' comfort but such freedom was ill-suited to everyday joinery in local timbers and the small joiner, with or without the help of the turner, continued to make extremely sound but massive little gateleg tables. These are so hardy that many have survived to this day and have been augmented by generation after generation of similarly minded craftsmen.

Those made this century may have the ugly black staining of would-be antique oak and are often assembled from machine-shaped parts with a minimum of careful finish, but basically they differ little from those made by hard hand labour nearly 300 years ago. A narrow rectangular top, on normal under framing and four corner legs linked by stretchers, has flaps hinged to its long sides. These hang down close to the framing but can be lifted level with the table top and supported on extra legs that swing out, pivoted between underframing and stretchers. Sometimes there is only one flap and sometimes each flap is so wide that two legs are required to support it. The resultant table may be oval, round or rectangular, the flaps sometimes hanging almost to the floor. Sometimes, too, there is a small drawer in the underframing: this runs on a central bearer as the side framing is required for the pivoting gatelegs.

An old circular cottage table that I covet has a top a full 36 inches across, cut from a single piece of timber, but usually the joiner had to make the best of narrow boards. When good timber was available he indicated its strength, and made the table easier to handle, by cutting the top very thin. At first the edge of the top was cut square on all sides but later in the 17th century this was more often rounded and from this came the idea of "softening" the edge, cutting it back on the underside to make it appear even thinner.

The edge was never carved, except on late 18th-century spider tables and in Victorian or later "Tudor". But from the late 17th century the joiner experimented with alternatives to the square edges where the fixed top joined the flaps. A short-lived method was a narrow tongue on each flap fitting a groove in the edge of the fixed top. But this was bettered in the rule joint where convex thumb moulding along the fixed top was matched by concave moulding on the flaps. By this arrangement, even when the table is closed, there are no ugly gaps between the top and the hanging flaps and the hinges remain out of sight.

The legs of these tables are fascinating to anyone interested in what the turner could achieve with his primitive lathe, although no very definite dating can be ascribed to the various outlines. All the familiar styles were in use during the 17th century though it is usual to attribute the mediocre ball and reel repeats to mid-century work and more adventurous twists and balusters to the more sophisticated late Stuart years when native craftsmen were challenged by tiresomely enterprising foreigners and when more amenable walnut ousted tough oak from fashionable use.

Some of the earliest legs are almost plain upward-tapering rods and slightly reeded columns have been dated to the early 17th century. Thereafter the different individual turners produced a fascinating assortment of ball and bobbin patterns and more shapely balusters. Inevitably there remains, too, a certain amount of the gaudy swash or twist turning that invaded us from the Continent in Charles II's day, although in table legs the tendency was to introduce no more than a few turns in a pillar mainly composed of substantial vase or baluster outlines. The last years of the 17th century saw some extremely rich shaping in the cup and trumpet and Portuguese swell at knee height on expensive walnut writing tables and this style of rounded knee and downward tapering outline for the main feature in the leg turning appears, too, on these gateleg tables, although in modified, timber-saving form.

The turnery may end with the square block required for tenoning the stretchers, but in good work there is usually a ball or bun foot below and occasionally a carved foot such as the bent-under scrolling fist effect, known as the Spanish foot. In good work, too, the stretchers, including those on the pivoting legs, are turned to harmonize, but on a small table they are often plain. In any case both the long fixed stretchers and the pivoting legs have to be left square where they are halved for fitting neatly into each other when the table is closed.

Perhaps the most interesting style to us today is the table

48

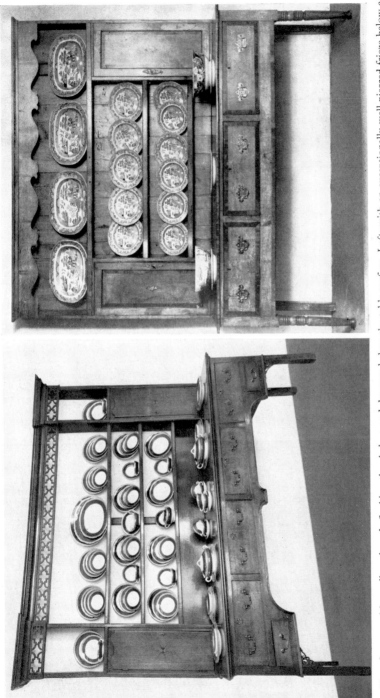

7. Two dressers with small cupboards flanking the shelves and drawers below the table surface. *Left:* with an exceptionally well-pierced frieze below a dentil moulded cornice. The cupboard doors have the double arch shaping found on many a long case clock and star inlay in contrasting woods. *Right:* with cupboards ornamented with the shell motif introduced on much late 18th-century provincial furniture and drawers cross-banded in mahogany.

8. The upper chest dates to about 1630 but shows a primitive form of construction with the massive front and back planks nailed to vertical end planks extended to form feet. The lock plate suggests a later replacement, a frequent hazard among antiques with metal mounts. The lower chest, although dated to the 16th century, shows a more elaborate constructional technique. This has the heavy canted lid of some medieval chests but the front is of panels held loosely by the framework composed of vertical corner stiles, intervening muntins and horizontal rails joined together by mortise-and-tenon joints. In this example construction is complicated by the fact that the piece is made to be dismantled for storing flat by removing the pegs at front and back.

which the joiner has constructed with little or no help from the turner. This contains features inherited from the early trestle table. The fixed central section of the table is supported on flat, solid trestle ends, shaped to an ornamental profile and rising from trestle feet that are often little more than plain blocks of wood. These are linked an inch or two above the floor by a base board or a pair of flat stretchers supporting the lower ends of the gatelegs' inner uprights. Sometimes the legs themselves are turned but in the most interesting of these tables these, too, are flat bars of wood, also cut in ornamental profile. Thus the whole effect at a glance is of a turner's table.

Most popular, probably, was the simple, wavy outline suggesting once-new and presumably costly twist turning. Always, of course, at this time the pricing of work depended far more upon the cost of materials than upon the tiny outlay per man-hour of labour, and substantial boards in slightly undulating outline could be of much cheaper wood than was needed for delicate turnery.

All these styles continued to some extent far into the 18th century but soon dropped out of the fashion records. For dining, with the establishment of heavy Honduras mahogany, the table of fashion was the simpler gate table and this with various types of leg is illustrated on trade cards throughout the rest of the 18th century. Here part of the underframing on each side of the fixed central table is hinged to swing out, complete with a stretcher-free leg. This leaves a leg and a tiresome piece of underframing under each of two diametrically opposite corners of the fixed table top and a leg under the centre of each flap. For occasional use there was also the Pembroke type of little table with one or two bracket supports swinging out from the underframing to take the weight of what are narrow flaps, usually round-cornered. But this, too, is a dressy, rich little piece of furniture. Its successor was the flap-ended sofa table.

More everyday work for middling families is found among the various pillar and claw tables made in great abundance through the second half of the 18th century. Here again was work for the turner. A trade card of about

1770, issued by William Russell "Mahogany Turner and Cabinet Maker" of Fetter Lane, London, illustrates a round table with three fixed legs and one hanging flap on an extra hinged leg, a round gate table, a pillar and claw table and a three-tier pillar and claw dumb waiter. Even these may seem too sophisticated for modern ideas of cottage furnishings, but it is interesting to note that Loudon specifically refers to dumb waiters among his cottage, farm and villa furniture in 1833, as suitable for small farmers, bailiffs, country tradesmen and the like.

Assuredly such furniture is far more homely than the last fashion phase of the gateleg table which was an entirely delightful little piece but as uncountrified as a beribboned poodle. These tables of the 1760s–70s show the gateleg construction reduced to extremely slender proportions. The legs and stretchers are in a strong wood, such as mahogany, usually plainly turned but left square for all jointing and raised on daintily turned feet. The top may be mahogany, yew or other decorative wood; sometimes the whole table is in satinwood. Sometimes there is only one flap and on the other side corner stretchers give more space for the sitter's feet. In the 19th century some small gateleg tables were known as Sutherland tables. In this design the fixed top was very narrow in proportion to the deep flaps.

In the early 19th century, however, demand for plain commonsense furniture such as gateleg tables was far stronger than some tyro collectors imagine. Comment a hundred years ago marvelled at people's willingness to choose cottage furniture in oak and stained deal of a fundamental plainness that cost them more than pretentious mahogany.

Chapter Five

LONG CASE CLOCKS

SEVENTEENTH-CENTURY long case clocks are
slender exquisites but also specialist collectors' rarities.
They certainly have no place in the cottage, though often
their unpretentious style may better suit modern notions of
cottage furnishings than the carved mahogany grandeur
of the 1760s. Through the 18th century these most companionable clocks underwent many changes. Those no longer
wanted by fashion found welcome refuge in less pretentious
homes. But it is not always realized that in this quicker-
moving century they were augmented by ever increasing
numbers of clocks specifically made for workaday households—for the halls and kitchens of farmhouse and
merchant's villa—and these more especially tended to
become eventually the clocks of the cottagers.

These were made well into the 19th century in styles
so simple and straightforward that often they are thought
to date from George I's reign rather than George IV's.
Yet throughout the same period clocks were produced that
bear no relation to the cheaper types. The majority, it
appears, were regulator timepieces for large establishments
where exact time was beginning to be of some importance.
Clock makers and repairers needed them too for setting
and testing their own less meticulous stock in trade. But
the rest of us today may be misled in our dating by their
almost startling outward simplicity.

In this survey, therefore, I propose to begin no earlier
than George I's arrival on the throne in 1714 but to consider
in some detail the range of long case clocks being made
concurrently through the early, middle and late 18th
century and continuing into the 19th. Then by looking

51

at a clock the beginner collector can have some idea both as to when it was made and for what sort of market. It goes without saying that far greater knowledge would be needed to assess the clock's working parts. Alterations to the mechanism often go far beyond the scope of legitimate repairs and sometimes the maker's name upon the face is a century older than what makes it tick. Clocks that have been deliberately restored to "mint condition", obliterating earlier alterations, are of course most dangerous of all. Books are available for such specialist study.

Nevertheless the outward appearance counts for much in a piece of furniture as attractive as a long case clock and its owner should pay it the compliment of careful scrutiny. From as early as the 1690s the law had required that a clock should show upon its face the name of its maker and his place of abode. Doubtless many clocks remained anonymous, but those that have survived have tended to acquire the names of famous makers and it is rare indeed today to find an English long case without a name. This is extremely useful to the tyro collector, for many thousands of makers have been listed with their working dates—for instance, in G. H. Baillie's *Watchmakers and Clockmakers of the World*.

When a maker's dates are known a considerable number of clues may be detected to check authenticity of hood and dial, body and base, to appreciate where a maker was an innovator and where he was content with time-worn methods. For the enthusiast, a more intensive study of many specimens may prompt an interest in regional differences, for here more than in most kinds of furniture it is possible to trace regional preferences, from Whitehaven to Barnstaple, from Port Glasgow to Wolverhampton. Newcastle, Bristol and Plymouth were especially renowned for their clocks in the 18th century.

Everyone knows the general appearance of the earliest long case or coffin clock, made from the 1660s. This was a graceful little clock six to seven feet tall but slender, composed of a simple hood with straight or gable pediment protecting the movement and a dial no more than about 9 inches across, a long narrow body for the passage of the weights and the swing of the pendulum and a squarish

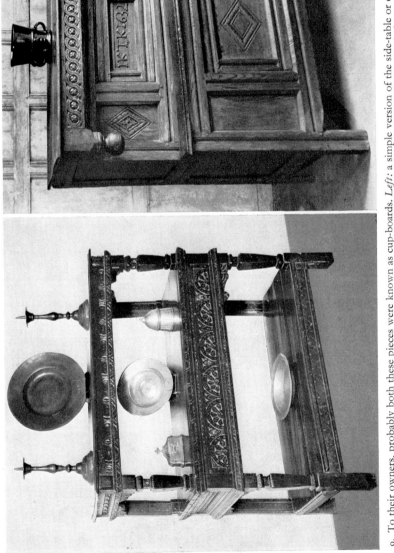

9. To their owners, probably both these pieces were known as cup-boards. *Left*: a simple version of the side-table or cup-board used for serving drinks and displaying family plate, in the tiered design known as a court or short cup-board. *Right*: also in simple form, a hall or parlour cupboard, showing guilloche and lozenge patterns popular in the 17th century.

10. Corner cupboards that indicate the range of this particularly accommodating furnishing. *Left*: an ornate panelled oak hanging cupboard of the 1760s. *Centre*: the glazed hanging cupboard associated with mahogany but here more individualistically expressed with handsome burr veneers of the countryman's yew wood. *Right*: two-tier type, its finely-grained oak ornamented with mouldings of damson wood.

plinth with deep base moulding. All too soon ebony veneer and ebonized polished pearwood were outmoded by surfaces of marquetry in the Dutch manner.

Early marquetry patterns of multi-coloured flower groups suggest foreign workmanship, but these soon gave way to scrolling arabesques in two or three contrasting wood tones and the intricate fragmentary two-tone patterns now known as seaweed or endive. Because of later developments it may be worth mentioning in passing that in the later 17th century the simple hood outline was lost to some extent, the classic pilastered pediment giving place to carved cresting in the crown-and-amorini style of much Charles II furniture, supported by twist turning. The silhouette of the cresting much resembles the scrolling arches of typical mid-Georgian clocks but detail of treatment is altogether different. As for the period's ubiquitous twist-turned columns—in fact three-quarter pilasters at the front and quarter-pilasters at the rear—in their Victorian rediscovery they were invariably made to "balance", with opposing twists.

At the time such details were soon forgotten, however, but the more sophisticated styles of marquetry continued into Georgian days, rivalled by simpler walnut veneers, including splendid burr walnut. Here, then, was the earliest style of Georgian long case clock. This was the period when great efforts were made to accommodate the clock to the lofty rooms of early Georgian affluence. At first it maintained much of its original feature detail, but with ever-increasing height and proportionate effect of grandeur. The hood continued the squarish outline but above the square dial rose tier upon tier of moulding. This superstructure is usually known as cushion moulding although one or more tiers may be in concave rather than convex outline. Two finials or three, such as ball-spires added yet greater height and the whole clock might be 8 or 9 feet tall.

At this time too, however, many a big house had a long case clock in a less pretentious room better suited to its proportions. Here an engaging vogue of the period was the flamboyant use of Oriental lacquers and the English imitation known as japanning. Long case clocks vividly japanned red, blue, green, yellow, black or cream may date to this period but the notion was in and out of fashion for minor rooms through much of the century and other features must aid in dating.

The earliest style of this ornament tends to show small isolated motifs painted upon the bright ground. In George I's reign and into the 1740s some imported Oriental lacquer boards were used for body doors, including designs in high relief. But the flatter English version of these rich medleys may date between 1720 and 1800 with emphasis on the period 1730–60.

Oak might be used for the carcase at this period but seldom is noted as the visible wood. Under japanning it was seldom satisfactory for large areas unless first veneered and even as a basis for veneer was never wholly suitable, as it tended to case-harden rather than to weather. Nor, it may be argued, was japanning particularly suited to the working clock and it tends to look shabby today unless heavily restored.

As regards clock case construction, the early hood had lifted off for access to the dial and when this became impracticable around 1690 it had been made to slide forward, but the obvious advance with more massive structures was the hood door. Designers retained the early three-quarter pilasters flanking the square of glass and hinged the whole front upon pins projecting from above and below. There might still be rectangles of glass in the sides of the hood, too, for viewing the movement and curiosity, or legitimate doubts about reliability, were met by a small round bob glass in the body door for glimpsing the swing of the pendulum.

From as early as the 1670s it had been necessary to accommodate a long royal pendulum with a one-second beat instead of the earliest short bob, but the early Georgian body is still well proportioned. The plain body door is square topped and, in good work, neatly edged with cross banding or lines of feather marquetry mitred at the corners, a detail English craftsmen were careful to observe. By 1715 it was becoming usual for mouldings in corresponding outline to link hood with body and body with base.

The most important part, the dial, is delightful on the early Georgian clock. It was cut from latten plate and soon established as a 12-inch square. The hour ring surrounds a central area matted to serve as foil to shapely hands, the hour hand with a spade design finely pierced and carved by cut-steel workers, the minute hand a long slender pointer on an S-shaped shoulder. Outside the hour ring four cast spandrels fill the corners, occasionally linked by engraved detail when the wood is closely patterned with marquetry. Occasionally, too, engraved ornament entirely replaces the spandrels. These had begun as simple winged cherub heads but had been elaborated into somewhat confused amorini and crown motifs.

In the silvered hour ring the large roman numerals may be separated by fleur-de-lis or other formal motifs and edged with arabic figures at five-minute intervals and in addition small pointers between the minutes may divide the hour into quarters. The dial within the hour ring is often further burdened with a small seconds dial and a square date aperture set within engraved ornament. The winding holes had become conspicuous details by Georgian days, edged with bright rings of brass to protect the matted surface around them from careless handling and incidentally drawing attention to the fact that the clock had a striking movement on an eight-day or even a monthly winding mechanism. Far apart winding holes and much bigger, heavier weights indicate the more complicated monthly movement.

In either case to be complete the early winding holes— some to as late as about 1740—have small covers, details now often missing or "restored". This bolt-and-shutter arrangement made it necessary for the winder to pull a cord and so set in motion a "maintaining power" mechanism before he could insert the winding key; without this maintaining power the clock stood still while being wound, as is the case with most of the everyday specimens more often encountered today. A maker's name and town, usually flanking the figure VI, complete the rich clock's dial.

The dial in a less splendid specimen of this time may show no winding holes, being wound daily by pulling up the weights; it may be a silent timepiece with a single weight; it may indicate the time with no more than a single hand. It cannot be stressed too often that these features all continued throughout the long fashion for long case clocks.

So much for the earliest Georgian style but about 1720 a change of dial affected the whole design: for greater height the dial itself acquired an arched top, low at first but eventually becoming a full half-circle. For the hood pediment this meant the rounded arch, variously moulded, that was the dominant feature of early 18th-century furniture, frequently "broken" to flank a still higher finial. At its most impressive of all such a high rounded arch, complete with corner finials, may be surmounted by still more flat-topped cushion moulding. For the front of the hood it meant an arched door more easily achieved by making it independent of the corner supports which thereupon were changed to fully rounded brasscapped pillars. For the body it meant a door with a slightly arched top to harmonize.

On the dial itself little enough use was made at first of the extra space where as often as not additional spandrel ornament of scrolls, dolphins and the like flanks an escutcheon containing the maker's name. Alternatively a date dial may be found there and the maker's name appear within the hour ring below the hands. The hour ring itself may retain its various divisions: the quarter-hour marks were the first to go. But the arabic minute figures of this period are inexplicably large.

By the 1740s–50s, however, that half-circle over the dial was becoming an intriguing detail on some long case clocks. The most obvious and long popular showed the moon's phases set in a starry sky: a member of the Ellicott family in about the 1740s introduced a half-dark moon in the round moving on a vertical axis, but then he even experimented with a barometer in the body. The usual method of showing the moon's phases was to have a revolving plate painted with two bland moon faces which rose and sank behind semi-circular obstructions—usually marked as terrestrial globes. Early moons have attractive sky settings; later there was a tendency to present a painted scene when the moon was new.

Once the moon took possession of this arch all kinds of supplementary information might be given such as tide times, usually with an interesting local basis. Animated figures, ships rocking on the waves and other amiable little entertainments are to be found, too, operated by the pendulum. Spandrels round the silvered hour ring tend to lack the earlier confident design, becoming somewhat inarticulate confusions of scrolling. Some are composed of scroll-flanked masks and others of urn and flower motifs. The crown-and-amorini design acquired crossed sceptres, but by the 1750s there was a general preference for asymmetrical rococo scrolling.

Much of the confusion of motifs between the figures was lost at this time, however, and the hour hand itself appears less richly ornamented, although the minute hand may show a somewhat spindly collection of opposing open scrolls. There may be a seconds ring above the hands and a crescent aperture for the date below. But occasionally, as early as the mid-century, all four hands—hour, minute, second and date—worked from the centre and used appropriate markings on the hour ring, the second hand being especially slender with a considerable counterpoise. The same method has been noted on Birmingham clocks of the 1800s.

The long case clock as a major status symbol in the middling rich merchant's home may be considered to date from the 1750s onwards. Chippendale illustrated ornate designs that tended to be rendered in broader and more massive outline in response to Midlands and North Country demands. In the earlier tradition of japanned casing the hood developed the curious pagoda outlines with deeply concave mouldings slanting up to a small central dome; here the body outline remains plain to set off its rich surface ornament. But the most impressive of these clocks are cased in veneers of mahogany, especially the wonderful fiery curl mahogany of the 1760s–70s. The classic proportions that appeal to the aesthete had been lost, but at their best some of these clocks through the third quarter of the 18th century show superb workmanship.

The characteristic hood outline has the swan-neck broken pediment or a modification of this in arching scrolls that culminate in roses or patarae, in carved wood or machine stamped brass, flanking a central pedestal for a vase or other gilded finial. The whole style of the clock can be judged by the rich treatment of this arching cornice, which may be intricately carved in low relief or filled with applied frets, the scrolls edged with dentil moulding, their paterae deeply carved. More carvings or applied frets link hood and body; by the 1770s the familiar pendant peardrop moulding was often used. A specimen by Benson of Whitehaven, dated by the Victoria and Albert Museum to about 1760, shows gilded blue glass under the scrolls and offers fascinating information regarding moon phases, daybreak, twilight and much else in the arch.

This arch may extend almost the full width of the square dial below and width here is increased to compensate by setting the hood pillars well away from the door. These may be rounded but often are in elaborate cluster-column form. At the back of the hood where the early maker had introduced quarter pilasters the mid-Georgian placed a flat board cut in cyma outline so that the whole clock hood, viewed from the front, suggests a double curve profile in keeping with the period's other bombé furniture. At the end of the century reeded pillars were echoed in reeding on the hood door and at the rear.

Below, the wide body—shorter and therefore much squarer than formerly—and the wider base establishes the clock's assertive tone. The top of the body door acquired an elaborate curved silhouette and to the sides of the door canted corners may be filled with pillars in similar style to those of the hood. The base has in-cut canted corners too, and sometimes a raised panel following the outline of the body door. To complete the base, small out-jutting feet are shaped in the swelling bracket outline of their day. Many of the cheaper clocks in oak cases date to this period, the oak sometimes uneasily edged with bandings of walnut or mahogany. The wood is most interesting when its potential as solid wood is emphasized in an era of veneers: deep carving on the hood, raised beading on the body door, raised panelling on lower body and base all give the plain wood an attractive country air.

The dial at this time was most often a single latten plate without a separate hour ring and often this appears silvered all over; cast brass dial plates were introduced from the mid-1770s. The spandrels from 1770 might be cast in the richly golden Emerson brass (see Chapter Thirteen), but in the costliest work continued in the fine alloy known as prince's metal, with their detail chased and engraved in a limited number of patterns that suggest a specialist supplier. Sometimes spandrel ornaments as well as the numerals were engraved on the flat silvered plate. Minute figures were reduced to the quarter-hours although large five-minute figures were still acceptable. Already by the 1780s there was some liking for the end-of-century style of symmetrical dials and pointers for the seconds and the date.

An important alternative for the dial, from as early as the 1750s, was the copper plate entirely covered with white enamel—creamy toned at first but really white from the 1780s. Here it is important to realize that this was merely an alternative and did not oust the silvered brass. The most obvious consequence came in the 1790s at a time of copper shortage with the introduction of dials of white-painted iron. Here again the collector may regard the change from silver face to white as deplorable, but at the time it was approved for bringing colour on to the dial where before it had been restricted to the motifs in the arch above.

On the white ground the corner spandrels could be replaced by full colour painting, producing the inevitable Elements, Seasons, Continents and similar appropriate foursomes. By then the maker's name might appear across the centre of the dial immediately below the hands. The hands themselves may show the period's new liking for matching detail, the minute hand being a simplified version of the somewhat spindly silhouetted curves covering the full length of the hour hand and strengthening what would otherwise be a flimsy article, being stamped from thin steel.

Some clocks from about 1770 produce not only chimes but tunes (and incidentally it may be mentioned that the so-called Westminster chimes may be assumed to be 19th-century work). The clock may play a tune at every hour or some other fixed interval, the tune selector and the strike-silent indicator usually being placed in the arch. One late 18th-century notion was the provision of tunes for weekdays and a hymn such as "O worship the King" for Sunday.

With the new delight in marquetry late in the 18th century some extremely ornate cases were lavishly enriched and this style has been noted well into the 19th century on somewhat squat North Country clocks. These are a far cry from the curving designs suggested in Sheraton's *Drawing Book* but he would approve the ovals, circles and fans of conventional marquetry and minor floral sprays on the cornice, all in woods of superb grain and colour.

Slightly less ambitious clocks towards the end of the century may be extremely attractive in detail. Carving on the hood may be replaced by simple lines of black-and-white chequers known as stringing, with perhaps a central motif of shell or flowers obtained complete from the specialist marquetry man, and this kind of ornament may be found even in the cheap little 30-hour pull-wind square faced cottage timepiece of this late period. Most conspicuous development at the century's end perhaps was the appearance almost for the first time of round-faced long case clocks with no dial space beyond the hour circle. The style had occasional 18th-century adherents, too: Nathaniel Brown of Manchester, for instance, produced some in the 1760s–70s and Richard Simister of Birmingham—with a moon aperture cut in the upper half of the circle.

By the 19th century the circular dial was often topped by a serpentine hood silhouette of a slightly gabled undulation. But, as I have said earlier in this survey, the high-quality specimens of this period were mainly regulator timepieces, intended for work and not at all for show and for that very reason, perhaps, doubly attractive to modern eyes.

11. Three developments of the folding gateleg table. *Upper left:* an early 17th-century example which opens to make a circular table, the flap resting on a hinged leg at the back. But one feels that its main purpose was as a side table. *Upper right:* a late 17th-century table showing the simplest form of single gateleg in walnut with baluster turning on legs and stretchers and the period's sophisticated Spanish foot. *Below:* the countryman's late 17th-century version of the fully developed gateleg table. The frame is of oak and the massive top of yew wood.

12a. The large gateleg table for family dining as it evolved in the late 17th century. Here the wide rectangular flaps require a pair of gatelegs each. There is a drawer in the framing, running on a central bearer, and the baluster-turned legs on ball feet are linked by moulded stretchers.

12b. The 17th century's love of reel or bobbin turnery is expressed in this museum specimen of the third quarter of the century. Under the open flap can be seen the gap in the underframing and its applied moulding shaped to receive the halved top of the gateleg with similar shaping in the stretcher below.

Chapter Six

SPINNING WHEELS

FOR sheer self-assurance few cottage furnishings can
rival the spinning wheel. Here is the unchallengeable
taskmaster of industrious countrywomen down the
centuries, every handsome detail directly purposeful, from
the sisters and the mother-of-all beside the wheel to the
stout three-legged base that maintained a firm stance on the
uneven cottage floor. Spinning was known in Bronze Age
Britain and the basic principle was elaborated into a wheel-
operated process practised in England at least as early as
the 14th century. The early 14th-century English illuminated
Decretals of Gregory IX, now in the British Museum,
illustrate a simple spinning wheel that differs scarcely at all
from many in commercial use more than 400 years later.

During these centuries time-saving improvements were
introduced although they never became universal and in
the 18th century many a fine lady found delight in spinning
as a pastime on the immensely decorative wheels that are the
collector's ideal today. Romney's portrait of Emma Hart,
Lady Hamilton, as a spinstress in this romantic mood is an
intriguingly accurate study of a spinning wheel. But
Chaucer in the Wife of Bath's Prologue (*c.* 1386) more
shrewdly saw spinning as a wearisome necessity:

> Deceit, weeping, spinning God hath given
> To Women kindly, while that they may liven.

The wheel speeded the cottager's work but even so more
often than not its hum must have seemed the song of a
tyrant, last heard in chorus, this century, in the still, humid
cellars where the ancient hand-craft far surpassed any
factory machinery in producing gossamer linen threads for

Edwardian finery. Today no more than an occasional wheel will be found in use, probably producing woollen yarn for hand knitting. But the wheels themselves may be met with from time to time and for the tradition-loving collector there is immense pleasure in ensuring that such a piece is complete and in working order before it takes as of right its place of honour in the cottage living room.

Innumerable ancient townships testify in splendid church and mansion to the world renown of medieval English woollen cloths, and it was wool that largely occupied the cottage spinster, although there are records in plenty of women spinners preparing their retted flax stalk fibres—first with scutching knife and block and then with hackling comb to make them amenable to spinning. In the Howard accounts of the 1620s, for instance, "a spinner and a carder [for wool] for a month" were paid 3s. 4d. in addition to their keep; another time three women heckling flax for 9 days were paid 2s. 3d

Flax spinning was vastly important to much of Europe and it was from Continental immigrants that England gradually adopted improvements to the wheel. But one of the delights of this ancient tool is the fact that in principle it is the same as the distaff and spindle that instilled in women the urge to be busy-fingered, no matter what their preoccupations, ever since thread was first required to transform skins into civilized apparel.

Experienced men and women wove the thread into cloth on hand looms and many an old record notes the arrival of the travelling professional weaver to work up the thread prepared in the evenings and at other spare moments by the girls of the establishment, the spinsters. When Kay's flying shuttle speeded weaving from the 1730s it took ten spinners to keep a weaver busy. Antony Fitzherbert in his *Book of Husbandrie*, 1523, noted complacently that "a woman cannot get her living honestly by spinning on the distaff but it stoppeth a gap and saveth her from being idle and the product was needful". He stressed that no rank was above the use of the spindle: "Princesses only have them gilt." Henrietta Maria's thrifty French servants were condemned in the following mid-century for teaching her spinning among other base employments, but Queen Victoria did not disdain to become skilful in spinning flax.

Fitzherbert pictures the lady carrying her distaff in her girdle and her spindle in her hand when spending half a day with a neighbour and "the farmer's wife with her maids about her in the evening, all spinning". Such a picture was confirmed, for example, by that stern housewife, Lady Grisell Baillie, whose *Directions to Servants*, 1743, laid down that laundry maids were to be "kept close at spinning till nine at night when they are not washing or other necessary work".

It is easiest to understand the working of a spinning wheel by envisaging how it developed from simple distaff and spindle. The wool had to be scoured, washed and usually dyed. But the most important preliminary was the carding, applied to cotton too and the short-staple portion of flax (tow). This is sometimes confused with the skilled combing involved in the preparation of long-staple woollen fibres used for worsted and most fibres of flax. In fact it was the reverse, since its purpose was to ensure the greatest possible subdivision and thorough random mixing of the fibres to obtain a coherent fluffy mass. This for convenience could be attached loosely to the distaff, a hand staff that, at its simplest, was merely a cleft stick about 3 feet long; some were handsome pieces of carving with loops to secure the wool. The distaff was held under the left arm or tucked into the belt, leaving the hands free for drawing out the wool or other fibre, wisp by wisp, from the loose bundle and twisting it into the beginnings of a continuous thread.

This thread was attached near the upper end of the other piece of equipment, the spindle—and spindle whorls have been found among the remains of our most ancient fore-bears at Glastonbury. The spindle was a slender rod, used hanging vertically, eight to ten inches long, tapering towards the ends and turned from wood or bone with a small perforated whorl of wood or stone near the lower end to provide momentum when it was briskly twirled. It was important that the weight should not be heavy enough to break the thread but equally important that it should keep

the spindle gyrating as long as possible, for it could never
be allowed to stop and reverse its spin.

Thus the spinner drew and twisted the fibres from the
distaff with her fingers and at the same time kept the dangling
spindle whirling so that, combined with the pull of the
weight, it made the loose hairs or fibres continuously turn
in upon themselves to cohere and make the more or less
even thread. It was a laborious method, of course, for the
spinner had to pause frequently and wind the spun thread
upon the spindle and secure the end in a notch before
proceeding. After this, when the spindle was full, the thread
had to be wound off on to a bobbin or reel.

The spinning wheel at its most primitive merely improved
the twisting of the spindle. A narrow platform or bench was
mounted at the ends with vertical brackets. One pair
supported the wheel and the other, smaller, the spindle
placed horizontally, both usually running on box wood or
leather bearings. The wheel was grooved for a cord or belt
that linked it with a pulley on the spindle so that a light
touch on the wheel kept the spindle turning while the
spinner drew her wool or flax from her distaff mounted
beside and somewhat above it. Nottingham Corporation
Records refer to the English use of a spinning wheel in
1404: the *Book of Trades*, 1806, shows a woman at a primitive
wheel of this design. Pyne in one of his exquisite but
inaccurate little drawings dated 1805 shows a woman using
a wheel in similarly early style, although here all the members
are finely baluster-turned in the traditional 17th-century
manner that has tended to confuse the dating of spinning
wheels.

Usually the spinner on this simple wheel produced her
thread in two stages. First she transformed the soft fluffy
mass into what A. Ure in 1836 described as "a slightly
twisted porous cord called a roving". In a second operation
she stretched and twisted this cord into "a fine cohesive
thread". In each operation she used her left first finger and
thumb to hold the yarn at an angle to the horizontal spindle
and so extend the cord while with her right hand she
turned the wheel. Then when she had transformed the mass
of carding to the lightly twisted roving she reversed the

13. Long case clocks showing fashion changes through George II's and George III's reigns. *Left:* the movement by John Simpson in a case of walnut veneer—a transitional piece of about the 1730s with cushion moulded hood, the dial richly ornamented in spandrels and arch and the front pillars opening with the hood door. *Centre:* by the familiar George Monkes of Prescot, in flamboyant case of mahogany enriched with carvings, mouldings and finely balanced veneers. This dates to about the 1770s. It has a moon movement filling the wide arch. *Right:* by John Whitehurst, F.R.S., of Derby and London, a notable clock maker who died in 1788. This shows the period's love of carved detail from swan neck pediment down to swelling bracket feet and the change to a white enamelled dial.

14. Typical specimens of the handsome long case clocks produced in many provincial centres through the middle and later years of the 18th century, and by no means exceptionally ornate. All share the same style of massive towering hood, wide-arched dial flanked by fluted corner pillars, arching body door and broad base. *Left:* dating to about 1745–55, the movement by T. Wilmshurst of Deal, in a case of veneered walnut. *Centre:* dating to the third quarter of the 18th century, the movement by William Stevenson of Maidstone, Kent. The hood is in what is now known as pagoda shaping, the dial is silvered and ornament is restrained to lines of stringing on body and base. *Right:* movement by William Barker of Wigan in a carved mahogany case of about 1780.

spindle to clear it of the few twists on its blade, then turned it forward again to wind the roving into a "cop" on the body of the spindle. Then a new carding had to be joined on by twisting and the process repeated. From this roving in much the same way, bit by bit, she spun her yarn. The early spinning wheel, then, was a simple little affair: one in the *Shuttleworth Accounts*, 1617, cost 2*s.* 4*d.* "for the cook's wife".

So much for the way the spinner handled her short staple wools until about the 1760s. Cotton thread was made in a similar manner and the process formed the basis of Hargreave's spinning jenny that produced a number of threads simultaneously. But the spinning wheel as most of us know it today is the much more elaborate variant which enabled the spinner to produce a continuous thread by spinning and winding at the same time. This was the machine used for flax and for the longer staple wool made into worsteds which during the 18th century came to require thousands of men for its preliminary hand-combing into orderly arrangements of the fibres.

This major improvement in spinning wheel design came as early as the third quarter of the 15th century but appears to have become generally accepted in England and Ireland only in the 17th century. It is illustrated in the celebrated *Waldburg Hausbuch* of the late 1470s and credited at one time and another to Leonardo da Vinci and Johann Jürgen of Brunswick. Aubrey in his *Natural History of Wiltshire*, about 1697, noted the improvement in the craft of spinning in the past forty years so that "one pound of wool makes twice as much cloth (as to extent) as it did before the Civil Wars". As early as 1645 a woman in East Dereham, Norfolk, spun a pound of wool into a thread more than forty miles long, but this was later doubled by a Norwich spinner.

The great advance consisted primarily in the time it saved, however, for the spinner no longer had to pause and wind her arm's length of thread upon the spindle nor pause again to transfer her thread from spindle to reel or bobbin. Instead, the wheel that turned the spindle also turned a bobbin that could thus receive the thread as quickly as it was spun. The driving cord from the wheel passed over a pulley to revolve the spindle as before but now either the same cord doubled round the wheel again or a secondary one on the same wheel passed over a slightly smaller (and therefore quicker turning) pulley on a flanged bobbin running freely on the spindle. Now as she turned the wheel, and at the same time fed the spindle with the ever-twisting wool or flax that her quick fingers drew from the distaff, the woman could watch the made thread passing from the spindle to the faster turning bobbin.

To spread the thread evenly upon the bobbin it passed first to a winged or U-shaped arc above it called a flyer with a row of small hooks along it. When one part of the bobbin was full the spinner had only to pause for a second to transfer the thread to the next hook on the flyer and so fill the next part of the bobbin. The size of the reel or bobbin was a matter for endless confusion in calculating the amount of thread, however: only in Ireland was the matter simplified by allowing only two sizes, long and short.

The fact that the process was continuous meant that the spinner could not introduce the twist in the way that she had done on the simpler wheel with its intermittent motion. Instead she had to return to the old twisting method of the dangling spindle. The comparative speeds of the spindle and bobbin concerned the spinner since the bobbin became larger as it filled with thread and upset the relationship, to the detriment of the spun thread. This happened whether the bobbin turned slower or faster than the spindle. In the early 18th century Louis Crommelin, reporting on the Irish flax spinning, noted that in France and Flanders only one band linked the wheel with the pulley of the spindle; the bobbin, being loose upon the spindle, revolved by the pull of the spun yarn. To check the speed of the bobbin a drag or brake was applied by means of a string which was fixed to bear upon the bobbin groove, automatically increasing as the bobbin filled and tended to move too fast. Old paintings of spinning scenes confirm the difference in method as shown by the single or double line of cord from the big wheel.

Inevitably the cottager had homely names for the working parts of this well-proved tool: the twin supports containing

66

the horizontal spindle, flyer and bobbin suggested obvious opportunities for handsome turnery and were known as the sisters. When as a further improvement the whole arrangement of sisters and spindle was mounted on a T-shaped movable base, this became known as the mother-of-all. This was an important detail as by turning a screw the spinner could move the mother-of-all towards or away from the wheel and so obtain the right tension for the driving belt.

The distaff holding the wool or flax was known also as the rock and 7th January was widely accepted as St. Rock's Day, marking the end of the twelve-day Christmas interlude and prompting preparation, at least, for a return to the more prosaic music of the wheel:

> Partly work and partly play,
> Ye must on St. Distaff's Day.

The other obvious requirement of the early spinner was more freedom for manipulating her wool or flax by introducing a foot treadle to spin the big wheel. Although hand-turned wheels were illustrated in the early 19th century the treadle had reached Europe from China early in the 16th century and is illustrated, for example, in the Glockendon Bible, 1524. It was a simple detail, consisting merely of a vertical rod connecting the wheel with a foot pedal.

By the early years of the 17th century, therefore, the wheel could appear in the forms most familiar to us today. Of these perhaps the most frequently noted is the horizontal design often called the low or Irish wheel. This was a slight modification of the Dutch wheel and the similarity might be expected since the first wheels for spinning flax were brought to Ireland from Holland in the early 17th century by the Earl of Strafford.

This design brought the working parts of the wheel and mother-of-all close together to left and right of the spinner on a small substantial platform base, oval or rectangular, mounted on three or four legs with the foot treadle between them close to the ground. In the most familiar Dutch wheel the platform was similar but set aslant so that the top of the wheel was on a level with the spindle. The wheel's nearly vertical supports might repeat or elaborate on the handsome turnery lavished on the sisters. Further attractive turned detail of knop and baluster would then ornament the legs and the ten or twelve, sometimes fourteen, spokes of the wheel.

In the British Isles popular designs included an Irish variant peculiar to Antrim and Donegal, known as the castle, with a small wheel rising above tall legs. This may still be found in use for spinning wool. An alternative design was the Scottish or low wheel, found too in Germany. This was a space-saving shape with the wheel mounted on a low platform, square or circular, the legs short and widely splayed and two or four supporting arms prolonged so as to hold the spindle, flyer and bobbin almost directly above. Rising still higher was the distaff, sometimes dowelled into a short projecting arm which might well prove a weak point in the design. A shapely specimen of ivory-mounted mahogany in the Victoria and Albert Museum of about 1760 has a slender turned rosewood distaff rising to a height of 4 feet 3½ inches, more than twice the height of the wheel top. This is inscribed "Willm Mark, Aberdeen".

Mahogany spinning wheels are often so finely finished that they tend to suggest the aristocratic patronage of leisured ladies, but among more workaday specimens may be found a range of woods. Some of the sturdiest are of oak throughout and for such a purpose this wood never went out of favour. Its treatment may puzzle the unwary, however. A specimen at Knole, Kent, has what might be regarded as Stuart baluster turning on all members, combined with neo-classic flutings and paterae upon the rectangular platform that date it to the later 18th century.

A spinning wheel personally owned by Sir Richard Arkwright, one of the pioneers of spinning machines in the 1770s, and now in the Science Museum, shows the simplest style of bobbin turning associated with Cromwellian days. Some wheels were mainly of beech with oak legs to bear the brunt of the wear and boxwood to support wheel and spindle axles.

The early wheel itself was massive to reduce the risk of

warping, built from four solid arcs of wood by the wheel-wright. But when tough, pliant yew was forced into arching shapes by the windsor chair maker, his methods were adapted for making yew wood rims to considerably lighter wheels. Another specimen in the Victoria and Albert Museum has a wheel of metal, well proportioned to its slender tapering legs in satinwood-banded mahogany veneer of about 1790. Its height is 3 feet. Here, too, the maker is known—"John Planta, at Fulneck, near Leeds." The design includes another small refinement of the period, a drawer under the platform, and diagonal stretchers link the legs above the treadle.

Some of these drawing-room specimens are decorated with the shell and flower motifs of the specialist marquetry men or with lines of checker stringing in contrasting woods. Sometimes the wheel is set with small circles of ivory to twinkle as it spins. In Regency years brass inlay was used. Lady Allgood in the third quarter of the 18th century had a graceful little specimen with a small wheel on a spindled platform over four turned tapering legs specially made to while away the time as she travelled by coach. And that indefatigable craftswoman, Mrs. Delany, was in no way put out when Queen Charlotte herself "caught me at my spinning and made me spin on and give her a lesson, and I must say that she did it tolerably well for a Queen."

Chapter Seven

WORKADAY CHINA WARES

COLLECTORS tend to divide their ceramics into ornaments and useful wares. This to me seems nonsense. Until at least the 19th century ornaments as such were for the tiny minority. Those of fragile porcelains were locked in rich men's cabinets. Even in fine earthenwares, the colour-washed portrait models and classical figures by the Woods and their contemporaries were designed for an educated and discriminating taste. But the vast majority of our forebears, workaday folk whose survival depended upon a thrifty self-sufficiency, found abundant ornament perfectly suited to their living quarters in the cups and jugs and platters that served their meals and were stored between times upon the dresser racks where their bright colours and reflective glaze gleamed against the dark wood. Smoke-resistant, dust-free from constant use and reasonably durable, they were also easy to see in the dusky light and easy to understand in their forthright treatments of everyday themes.

Of all antiques for the cottage collector, yesterday's useful wares are probably the most decorative, interesting and abundantly available. Chosen at leisure down the years they may also be extraordinarily informative and certainly endearing. A cottager's furniture would be mainly inherited, soft furnishings reduced to a nondescript working minimum, wall pictures no more than an occasional tiny, ill-drawn print. But sooner or later most families replenished their supply of crockery in the manner of their own day, to please their own particular fancies. In following their notions through generation after generation a collector can put together an exceptionally interesting survey of the potter's craft. It is possible to see clearly the public's basic needs and to understand the potters' response in advancing techniques, not only in terms of service and durability but equally concerned with the acceptability of the colour and decoration that would make their wares sell.

This is made easy by the very fact that these useful wares had to be produced in quantity. Moreover the renowned individualism of the smaller potters and their reliance upon local highly conservative demand meant that primitive processes directly derived from the Middle Ages were still used on a commercial scale in the 19th century. Many useful ware techniques remain fundamental to manufacture and ornament to this day. The mistake is to assume, for instance, that all slip ware is "primitive" and must date to the 18th century or earlier, that common stonewares were ousted by the more refined creamware and pearl ware.

This survey can indicate when each new notion was evolved but it would be foolish indeed to suggest when any process was abandoned. This is where collectors fall back on a wider knowledge of their period and its moods. They give critical scrutiny to a vessel's design, decoration and purpose before coming to any conclusions. Even the most functional piece often declares its period because it is bound to reflect in minor detail the shape or texture or decorative mood of the more costly vessels then setting the fashion trend. Even the public's ideas of size changed conspicuously: in teapots and tea basins and saucers, to name but three examples.

One glance at a mug may set its period, almost irrespective of its fabric, and the same may be said of a serving jug, responsive to passing fashion in every detail of waistline, rim and handle. I can think of few more attractive orna-ments than a row of 18th- and 19th-century serving jugs. In a collection of mugs special rarities might include 17th-century slip ware, clayware, English delft. Or the collection might more likely begin with the 18th century, with its stonewares, marbled, buff and white salt-glazed, and the glowing metallic purple-brown of Nottingham ware; Wedgwood black basaltes, perhaps, and the buff-toned cane ware and of course, the late 18th century's painted and printed earthenwares; the 19th century's splendid japan patterns on octagonal mugs of Mason's ironstone ware, perhaps, and certainly copper lustre, in the low, wide Regency outline and the subsequent waisted silhouettes often found in the splotchy lustre known as Sunderland ware.

Even frog mugs could be included or make a collection of their own. The frog or toad climbing up the inside of the mug would be hand modelled on an 18th-century mug but in the 19th century the body was shaped in a mould and only the legs added by hand while the horrible hollow variant, designed to drench the drinker if it could no longer scare him, was an invention of about 1830. Needless to say copies abound.

To these the enthusiast may add mugs of porcelain, smooth to the lips. Often in the later 18th century these followed the tulip outlines of silver and the barrels of the century's end, a shape familiar too in glass, silver, Sheffield plate and associated with the potters of Caughley. As with all useful wares, in the 18th century's porcelains and the 19th century's tougher bone china, each specimen assuredly will record some aspect of minor decoration appropriate at that day for a wholly functional vessel.

The potter's techniques for making useful wares developed vastly in the early 18th century. The previous century's ornamental slip wares such as posset pots have a primitive splendour in their lines and dots of contrasting clays but everyday needs far into the 18th century were met by less ambitious brown-ware potters. Old directories indicate how numerous they were and how mediocre their products. Local clays baked in simple ovens might turn red or brown or buff but nearly all acquired a yellowish tone when impurities such as iron came in contact with the lead glaze needed to make the earthenware impervious to liquids.

The early potter's alternative method was to fire the same clays at a greater heat: this resulted in impervious stoneware but for a clean surface it was glazed with salt, giving it at best a somewhat rough, granular texture. A particularly attractive variant of this common brown stoneware is Nottingham ware, made from about 1690 to 1800 by methods evolved by James Morley. He coated his stoneware with an irony clay in the semi-liquid state known as slip. The effect of the salt glaze upon this rich brown slip was a surface smooth instead of mottled and with a characteristic metallic sheen almost suggesting pewter. The ware in varying qualities was made elsewhere in the region and some late in the 18th century was decorated with colours.

The story of evolving useful wares may be regarded as a natural progress to better selection and greater refinement of the ingredients—itself indicating a break from purely localized supplies—and improvements in the firing ovens giving greater heat more exactly controlled. But it is seen more interestingly perhaps as men's prolonged attempt to imitate the china ware of Tartary. What they wanted was wares with white grounds untinged by the processes of baking and glazing that could show ornament not in other earthy tones of clay but in the coveted Oriental blue. I deal in Chapter Ten with the eventual dominance of English blue-and-white patterns. But not everyone has realized, I suspect, how those costly Oriental porcelains, ardently collected and flamboyantly displayed from the late 17th century, obsessed the makers of ordinary wares as well as those who eventually evolved our various forms of porcelain.

Brown-ware men continued to flourish of course. Splendid brown stoneware was made in Derbyshire and elsewhere in the early 19th century before becoming a considerable art medium for craft enthusiasts later in the century. Slip ware potters, too, continued their age-old methods through the 19th century. Their mugs, plates, harvest jugs and the like are welcomed by collectors today, including the lovely zigzag stripes of Welsh ware pre-dating mechanical exactitude of stripe. I have written of both in some detail before.[1] Here I want to trace instead the main forward urge that gave yesterday's everyday families and today's collectors the pleasure of cleaner, smoother, less primitive and more pleasantly useful ware.

The first move came in the second half of the 17th century with the tin-enamelled earthenware known to Georgians as

[1] See *Small Antiques for the Collector*.

73

delft ware. Here the potter did not get rid of his everyday earthenware but covered it under a substantial layer of white enamel opacified with costly tin. This smooth powdery white surface separated the earthenware from the lead glaze. Upon it, under the glaze, he could paint decoration in blue and in the few other colours that were unaffected by the subsequent kiln firing required to harden the ware and glaze. This is tougher and more glassy than Dutch delft, less evenly coated with the enamel so that some tinge of colour from the impure earthenware may spoil its whiteness, but it was a beginning. When potters could make a sufficiently pure white pipeclay they might use this to cover their earthenware with an opaque white glaze: mistakenly, this cheaper faïence ware is sometimes now called English delft.

This whitening of the surface with refined white clay is the basis of the next important advances. One was the development of white stoneware. This was salt-glazed like the brown so that the surface has the characteristic texture but is a thin and even somewhat translucent ware, if also somewhat brittle. At the time it was the nearest yet to Oriental porcelains. John Astbury is credited with introducing the strength of flints, crushed and calcined, into his ware in about 1730 and by 1750 some sixty Staffordshire potters were making a limited range of useful wares. The surface made the ware unsuitable for the general run of table services such as tea cups and dinner plates so potters concentrated instead on table accessories that did not have to match anything—and how perfect, for the same reason, they are today.

In the mid-Georgian days when ideas of gracious living were spreading to ever widening social groups an unpretentious family could enrich their table with a sauceboat or pickle plate in the ware or a pot for tea or coffee. This might be white or painted with patterns in underglaze blue from the 1740s or in richly coloured enamels from the 1750s as delectably as porcelains. The ware could be moulded or cast in notably clear-cut relief patterns, a style that suited such individualistic pieces.

There is a suggestion of a silversmith's work about a white stoneware cream jug, for instance, moulded (in parts) to suggest a pair of scallop shells and mounted on three fussy little feet. But then cream jugs in the full range of useful wares are a joy to collect anyway, each so small and self-contained yet completely a part of the period that produced it. This stoneware rococo work was followed in contrast by the neo-classic grace of the late 18th century, the square style of the century's end, the early 19th century's squat, capacious little pitchers and the gradual return to high necked, vertical lines in early-Victorian work. Handles changed from sharp little curves to rounded loops, to unsweeping arches, then to square-shouldered bows, not to mention such curiosities as the serpents in Mason's ironstone wares.

Refined clay and flint, basis of white stoneware, was the basis too of the better earthenwares developed from this period. For these Enoch Booth of Tunstall is given much of the credit. By refining the local clay, by adding clay from Devon and Dorset and ground calcined flint, he produced a sound basic earthenware. But his stroke of genius was to adopt the porcelain maker's technique for his glazing, presumably under licence from the patentee, Thomas Frye of the Bow porcelain factory. Booth fired his ware to a porous biscuit state and then dipped it into a liquid glaze composed of powered lead, calcined flint, Cornish clay and water. For the first time a set of table ware could really match, the glaze even and lustrous. This cream-coloured earthenware pioneered the method for producing useful wares that has been followed ever since. On this basis of more refined ware and liquid glaze, Josiah Wedgwood forged ahead to produce his famous wares of the 1760s and 1770s. His cream ware made after 1764 has a harder glaze, its rich yellow tone showing an oily iridescence when held at an angle to the light, unmarred by any lines of crazing. He made every kind of table vessel and dish, some with relief ornament such as jessamine sprigs in the porcelain manner, some covered with the splendid variant of his yellow glaze now greatly sought as green glaze ware. This has its own long story of success.[1]

Cauliflower ware comes into the picture here, also with a

[1] See *More Small Decorative Antiques*.

range of teapots, coffee pots, sauceboats and all the subsidiary items outside the ordinary table service. These are naïvely shaped and coloured and moulded in relief to suggest cauliflower or pineapple. But some of the loveliest colouring in subdued smoky tones of slate blue, grey, green, dark brown and yellow is found in these earthenwares when the clear glaze is spread over powdered colour made with metallic oxides. These mingled in the firing process in what was known at the time as tortoiseshell ware. Wedgwood's early partner Thomas Whieldon is credited with this ware, introduced about 1750, and it continued to some extent into the 1820s.

Wedgwood was so pleased with his cream-coloured earthenware that he obtained Queen Charlotte's patronage and in 1765 it became queen's ware. But only in 1776 after legal wrangling was he able to make further improvements using the ingredients of his choice—Cornish china clay and china stone formerly monopolized under a patent that still restricted their use for porcelain.

This is 18th–century useful ware at its finest, far stronger than any earlier earthenwares and lighter in weight. Delft and white stoneware went right out of fashion but this improved cream ware was unassailable until the 1840s when production methods were modernized. By 1784 the *Staffordshire Directory* was listing 20 other makers including such familiar names as Wm. Adams, Josiah Wood, Thomas Wedgwood and John Bourne, but Josiah Wedgwood's greatest rival was the exceptionally light, finely glazed cream ware from the Leeds Pottery (1760–1821). A glance through the Leeds pattern books indicates the great range of table wares, the characteristic simple shapes. But it is a mistake to credit the firm with what were in fact fashionable details of their day common to all capable potters such as the most famous twisted handles attached by flower and leaf motifs. Leeds was sparing with colour and its fine black transfer-printed decoration (blue in the early 19th century) but produced superb pierced ornament, on chestnut baskets and their stands, the rims of plates and the like.

Many collectors seek the flawless yellowish glaze, the gourd and melon outlines and the exceptionally light bodies made by Leeds, their lightness, of course, aimed to cut weight-determined export costs. But others extend the field by concentrating on wares rather than on a single maker, choosing for example table baskets for chestnuts, fruit and so on. Leeds made these not only by piercing the ware in lacy patterns but by twisting and plaiting strips of clay, a job for a nimble-fingered child with an eye for symmetry. The collector soon discovers a variety of makers and techniques, culminating, far from the cottage shelf, in the shimmering mother-of-pearl glazed porcelain of mid-19th-century Belleek.

Success never slowed Wedgwood's passion for improvement. In 1779 he added more flint and more china clay to his cream ware and evolved his hard, tough pearl ware. This was a little yellow-tinged at first but became white by 1790 and proved ideal then for blue painting and printing. "New pearl ware" followed in 1809.

Wedgwood's fine-stonewares—basaltes, jaspers, red ware, cane ware—were made into many useful pieces including jugs, teapots, cups and saucers. For the cottage collector there is a particular charm in naïve use of cane-coloured fine-stoneware for covered pie-dishes made to resemble the decorative golden crusts of raised pies, a direct result of the flour tax caused by the Napoleonic wars. The Turners, Davenport and others made these magnificent-looking pies topped with crusty representations of dead game. The fashion continued and William Ridgway among others made them less expensively by moulding the relief work in the 1830s.

In Wedgwood's other fine-stonewares, however, the subdued colours and intense black with a velvety matt surface sought—successfully—to capture an educated public. The sprigged ornament was in the cultivated neo-classic mood and the alternative consisted of the wholly impersonal eccentric line work known as engine turning. This I find fascinating but it was a far cry indeed from the jolly sailors, plump-cheeked Britannias, cows and flowers, fantastic birds and sporting scenes that could be daubed in bright colours on the white earthenwares of the century's end.

Cottagers could brew their tea or serve their ale in Pratt

ware, for example, gay or gaudy according to taste. This form of decoration seems, in fact, to have been evolved by the younger Ralph Wood, not Felix Pratt, as a successor to delft ware in as far as it used colours that could be applied before glazing—high temperature colours. These included thick orange ochre, pale yellow, blue, green, purple-brown, often mottled or stippled. The ware was manufactured from about 1790 to the 1830s, Pratt making a lot of it from about 1803.

By the 1790s even the commonest brown earthenware might be turned into a splendid cottage ceramic by covering it with rockingham glaze. This was evolved at Rockingham but was applied by potters everywhere. It was merely a lead glaze heavily stained with manganese. The deep purple-brown was of varying intensity and softly iridescent, end-lessly popular for the old brown teapot and found too in dessert ware and the like. Jet ware deserves mention too, at its most appealing perhaps when touched with gilding. Its lustrous glaze was achieved with cobalt blue on brown earthenware fired in a smoky kiln. It was first made at Jackfield, Shropshire, in the 1750s–70s but it was produced in quantity in a harder earthenware by Staffordshire and at Alloa, for instance, in the mid 19th century and later and this is what usually comes to light.

Porcelains were made in England from the 1740s, first merely as imitations of the Chinese ware and eventually "true" or "hard paste" in the 1760s. But for the collector of useful wares the first porcelain that was tough as well as translucent, shining white yet not fabulously expensive, was bone china. This to most of us is china to this day. It was made by combining the hard-paste porcelain ingredients with calcined bone ash in the 1790s when the last monopoly of ingredients ended and the firm of Josiah Spode could go ahead with their splendid ware. They were closely followed by Minton, Davenport, Coalport, Liverpool; by Derby in about 1805, New Hall about 1810, Wedgwood from about 1812.

Spode also evolved a felspar porcelain in about 1800, very translucent, very hard and wonderfully flawless. This too was made by his rivals such as Coalport, Derby and Chamberlain of Worcester but was for costly tables. Bone china was sufficiently lovely for most of the newly genteel and this is the translucent ware found under the full range of decoration that makes the early 19th century a splendid hunting-ground for those who love colour, gaiety, iridescent surfaces, unassuming prettiness in pattern and shape. In Chapter Nine I consider the claims of copper lustre but some collectors prefer the platinum backgrounds of "silver resist" lustre or the gorgeous impossible detail of japan patterns. There was a spell of black decoration around 1830 but on the whole flowers were never richer, gilding never more admired—a splendid time for the extrovert.

The 19th century saw the rise of many huge potteries turning out vast quantities of bone china and high-quality earthenwares for table use. Time and again the collector finds the name of Adams, Ridgway, Meigh, Mayer and so on and far more wares with no more than the pattern names or numbers. Among the improved earthenwares Spode's stone china is found with his mark. This is a strong felspathic earthenware with a clear ringing tone introduced about 1805 and improved by 1810. It was twice as heavy as earthenware and slightly blue-grey in tone with a fine texture that did not need a mass of concealing decoration. Davenport, too, made some excellent stone china and other potters in varying qualities. Some makers can be identified including Wedgwood before 1825 and the Ridgway firm from 1814.

Semi-porcelain, opaque porcelain and similar misleading names date to this inventive era. All are improved earthenwares with some use of felspar instead of china clay—and nearly all desirable cottage wares today. Ironstone china is entirely different from stone china. This was patented in 1813 by Charles James Mason at a time when the top layer of the molten slag from the blast furnaces, a pale green glassy substance, could be ground to powder and used in this durable ware. Blast furnace processes changed in the 1840s but the name continued in use by Mason and his successors. Iron furnace slag was used for a time too in another tough ware known as lava ware. This was coloured in brown and purple and blue for heavy-handed cottage use: an "improved" variety was patented in 1852.

Yet another cottage ware of the period was called flint enamel ware, developed in the late 1840s, its solid weight due to a large proportion of powdered flint.

By then the well-to-do were rejoicing in the white effects of parian ware and the heat-resistant white stone-wares evolved in the 1830s but these surely were never for smoky cottage use. Colour in rich lustrous washes returned to favour in Minton's majolica ware from 1851. These blues and pinks, purples, greens and browns have a wonderful glowing depth, being applied over tin enamel on a basis of cane-coloured stoneware—later over parian ware. By the 1860s Minton and other potters were using domestic majolica for massive furnishings such as umbrella stands, wine coolers and jardinières but it may be found too in table wares such as dessert services, bread trays, candle-sticks, teapots and so on that are charming today.

For cottage collecting, however, there are innumerable wider quests. Teapots of course, or just rustic teapots with such delicious details as twiggy handles—crabstock to the near-countrymen who made them. Or mustard pots and pepper pots that can be found occasionally with the simple finger squiggles associated with banded ware, as well as in lustres, mocha (Chapter Eleven) and other homely styles. Or those tantalizing all-to-seldom complete food warmers that glimmered companionably at the bedside, or the jelly moulds with their central decorative cones and pyramids intended to prop up the wobbling jellies on the hot, candlelit table.

Few people as yet collect water filters yet these must have been invaluable in many a country household. There were no fewer than twenty exhibitors at the 1851 Exhibition and Doulton filters, for example, were marketed in a number of patterns to the end of the century. At one Portobello pottery in the 1830s, where only salt-glazed stoneware was made, the bucket-shaped water filters were thought worth decorating in high relief with hunting scenes, groups of men and women drinking, animals, flowers—an intriguing off-beat subject. Now, these handsome, lidded 5-gallon vessels with their abundance of decoration masking their homely purpose seem as remote as those dreaming days of Victorian summer that called for long cool drinks under the cedar trees.

15. Spinning wheels in contrasting designs. *Left:* low wheel, also known as the Scottish wheel. In this exceptionally graceful specimen the distaff is of turned rosewood, the wheel and platform of mahogany with ivory mounts but the design is that of many a Scottish crofter's specimen. Four vertical supports flanking the wheel hold the spindle, flyer and bobbin directly above it. The circular platform is small but is steadied by the widely splayed legs. The maker is noted as Willm. Mark, Aberdeen. *Right:* spinning wheel by John Planta, Fulneck, near Leeds. This too is a fine quality piece, its constructional style dating it to around 1790. The wheel is of metal and the platform, of table height, contains a drawer.

16a. The food warmer or veilleuse is a companionable little piece, decorative as well as useful. It was popular from the later 18th century and intended to ensure a warm drink for the restless sleeper. But the collector may have a long search to find one complete with the perforated stand, the lidded cup, often a second vessel to fit below this for hot water and at the bottom the essential open flame lamp. *Left:* in cream-coloured earthenware with a candle socket on the lid. *Right:* in fine stoneware with the attractively unobtrusive ornament known as engine turning.

16b. Staffordshire salt-glazed white stoneware of the mid-18th century showing the slightly mottled texture of the salt glazing that largely restricted its use to table accessories such as serving vessels. Typical of this clear-cut ware is the double-handled sauce boat in the silversmith's manner.

Chapter Eight

———

NOT so very long ago any trifling or amusing little fantasy for adult diversion was a toy. I have a particular liking for the variant "image toy" which perfectly calls to mind the kind of primitive little figure ornaments made in some numbers in England through the 18th century. These were far different from contemporaneous sophisticates in imported china ware or even the imitations of these in European porcelains. Eighteenth-century advances in techniques for making useful wares described in the last chapter gradually changed their style and each change produced examples that could make any collector ecstatic today. But now they are such costly rarities that few indeed can have a place among cottage antiques and I doubt if they ever did.

Here it is enough to show how far the craft had advanced by the beginning of the 19th century when earthenware potters lost their porcelain-minded pretentiousness and acquired a new quality of homeliness to meet a new class of purchaser. This was essentially a cheap market, the customers mainly country folk drawn to town life for factory employment. Their earnings might be niggardly, but with a little cash in their pockets they could ease their homesickness with reminders of country ways in the familiar tradition of the good-old-days-that-never-were.

These pieces may be regarded in a sense as peasant art in so far as they met the new-found needs of a workaday population eager, perhaps for the first time, to associate itself with the busy world around. They might give a local or human slant to wars and politics, sovereigns and celebrities, but were still more absorbed in the time-old matters of romance, sport, social custom. They were simple as the

6   81

innumerable models of mild-faced lions, sentimental as a Morland print. They altogether lack the traditions of functional grace that potters retained in their useful wares and may be dismissed by the purist as ugly little upstarts. Doubtless so were their owners when they sought to mitigate their drab surroundings with an arbour group of lovers under half a dozen oak leaves or a ewe with her lamb as naïve as those from Chelsea that had decorated rich dessert tables with pastoral fantasies nearly a century before.

By the end of the 18th century these earthenware figures were merely "toys", thus ranking with fragments of cheap costume jewellery and the like. But the 1830s they were firmly established as "chimney ornaments". The important potters of the late 18th century had kept mainly to the pretentious traditions of the porcelain figure makers, but technically the younger Ralph Wood (1748–95), Enoch Wood (at work 1783–1840) and their associates had vastly changed the manufacturing methods. It was this knowledge that made many comparatively insignificant potters of the early 19th century able to produce great quantities of extremely cheap little pieces, ugly, rough and ready, of poor ware hastily coloured, but then—as now—essentially lively and saleable.

As in useful wares, there was some continuation of primitive work through the 19th century, especially in hand-shaped slip ware from traditional regions. But the main current of development was with such potters as the younger Ralph Wood who fired his figures to the biscuit state, fired them again to fix their smooth white glaze—derived from the improved Greatbach glaze of 1764—and fired them yet again, but at a lower temperature, to fix the bright but sparse metallic oxide colours brush-painted over the glaze.

More cheaply he, and thereafter many others, applied the limited range of so-called high temperature colours to the figures in the once-fired biscuit state before glazing: this was the Pratt-ware of about 1790 to the 1830s. As mentioned in the previous chapter, the colours were limited to a dullish blue, pale yellow, thick ochre orange, olive green and purplish and greyish browns. They usually look somewhat opaque, though some potters tried to lighten the effect by stippling and mottling.

Such figures were part and parcel of the Potteries but they were made too in Sunderland and at the Herculaneum Pottery, Liverpool. They include, for instance, soldiers dating from the Napoleonic wars, reduced to extremely simple outlines for easy casting. Even these demonstrate a deterioration of technique in the interests of cost cutting, as all extraneous detail such as the gun was merged upon the basic supporting stump or prop rising from the plinth. Such a figure could be shaped by pressing or casting in a mould with a minimum of subsequent hand finishing.

The Woods worked mainly for middle-class homes, but some of their subjects are relevant to this survey because they reappear time and again in the early 19th century's more haphazard manner. Particular favourites include such Old Testament figures as Elijah with the raven and the Widow of Zarephath. These were made as a pair by Ralph Wood late in the 18th century. The sprigged decoration of their dress is in the expensive porcelain tradition, but the porcelain maker's triumphant absurdity, the background of flowering shrubbery known as a bocage, is reduced to the representational form of a few leaves and branches. This notion is often assumed to have been introduced to earthenware in the following century by John Walton. Inevitably Walton issued his own rough little version of the Widow and Elijah pair, as did Ralph Wood's cousin, Enoch Wood, in the 1820s.

Other enduring favourites include the woman with her broom and piece of silver from the New Testament parable and a gracious Charity group. This Charity with her two children had a varied career too, and is more often found than the companion figures, Peace with an olive branch and Hope with an anchor. All were designed originally for Wedgwood by Mrs. Landres and were made, for example, with some care by Leeds.

Small figures in another style that continued into the workaday world of the 19th century were made by Neale & Wilson, partners 1786–1801. These include carefully painted little Seasons. They were shaped in two-piece moulds instead of being cast and given a near-porcelain dignity with carefully made plinths, but their themes may be found time and again among early 19th-century potters. They were made by Thomas Rathbone of Portobello, for instance, again on tall plinths, and by some of the Sunderland potters and others. A rarity attributed to the firm is a figure at the British Museum covered entirely in silver lustre, produced at the period when lustred pottery was being offered to the thrifty as a cheap substitute for silver vessels. Silver (platinum) lustred figures are associated, too, with another Wood, Enoch's cousin Ephraim, with Elijah Mayer and the firm of Bailey & Batkin, all around 1820. Touches of copper lustre on dress and plinth are often noted on figures made by the Sunderland potters (see Chapter Nine).

Another late 18th-century partnership, that of Lakin & Poole, 1791–97, is remembered today for an imaginative "Assassination of Marat by Charlotte Cordé" rather than for its prestige work among classical figures. As makers of the "Tithe Pig" group—a woman offering her baby to the cleric while her husband holds on to the piglet—they illustrate the way a porcelain subject, long popular with Derby, could be adapted into the less exclusive class of ornament.

Leeds figures of this period are square-plinthed, cast hollow throughout as is seen in the hollow base (as distinct from a small hole) which shows glazing inside as well as outside. Some have the clean modelling and lustrous glazing of costly work, but some are restricted to the tones of blue, yellow, red and green that responded to the same kiln temperature and so could be fired together with a great saving of time and labour. Enoch Wood, associated with the late 18th-century developments in earthenware figures, continued the 18th century's figure traditions until 1840, producing such favourites as Elijah and the Widow, a sentimental "Widow and Orphans" and the humorous "Vicar and Moses" which shows the vicar slumbering in the pulpit while his clerk drones through the service.

So much for the background to those engagingly ugly little figures of the early 19th-century world, the lovers and lions, the "Tenderness" and "Friendship" that were soon jostled on the mantelshelf by hundreds of more immediately identifiable individuals. In this work, age as well as quality

17a. Jelly moulds are decorative little pieces of earthenware that often pass unrecognized. To be complete the mould requires two pieces. The jelly was poured into an inverted mould then a central core was inserted, point downwards. When set, the jelly was turned out complete with this decorative core which served to prop it up on the hot candlelit dessert table. Here, left and right, are two such cores, to fit square and round based jelly moulds. In the centre is a wedge-shaped core and also the mould that it was made to fit. These are Wedgwood queen's ware of about 1790.

17b. Wedgwood's cream-ware of the later 18th century is found in many delightful pieces for table use, the neatness of their outlines enhanced by the simplicity of their ornament. This cruet set is self-explanatory, its dish 11¼ inches long.

18. It is easy to understand the lasting appeal of many decorated useful wares. *Top:* these jugs in the bounteous shape popular around 1800 and well into the 19th century are in stoneware with ornament in low relief against a background wash of deep blue. This particular scene of men and horses is among the most popular of its day, introduced by John and William Turner and used also by Josiah Spode and his successor W. T. Copeland and by John Davenport of Longport. *Centre:* interesting specimens for the collector of frog mugs, with typical transfer-printed ornament. The loving cup bearing the date 1832 *(centre)* has lost its handles but not its content of no fewer than seven frogs. The Sunderland specimen *(right)* bears the maker's mark Moore & Co., Southwick. *Below:* the interiors of three mugs showing the frogs, two in the usual position to the side where they would remain concealed by the murky liquor until almost the end of the drink.

may be indicated by design. A pair of boxers, for instance, in Leeds City Art Gallery represent Tom Crib and Tom Molineux (Crib being world champion throughout the Regency) as carefully put together as if modelled in porcelain, the parts of the body separately moulded and built into poised aggressive little fighters. In contrast a two-part press-mould invented about 1830 made it easy to shape a suitable model in a single piece, plinth and all. In thin common ware this could be shaped, fired to a biscuit state, glazed and finally ornamented with a few overglaze colours both cheaply and acceptably.

What was lost gradually was the originality and liveliness of pose and the colour richness. Early 19th-century figures are as angularly lively as marionettes; Victorian flat-backs stand as stiff as early photographs and often with but little more colour.

Among the makers of these early 19th-century figures names are rare. This means that undue credit goes to the few who are known. It means, too, that a piece with a name such as Walton may be suspect. But then collectors of these cheap little wares must always be alert to the fact that they were easily made and are easily copied today. It cannot be stressed too often that thousands upon thousands of small figures were made for selling in factory towns, villages and fairgrounds and for carrying on great trays by hawkers through the streets.

Of the few who named the figures they made in this homelier early 19th-century manner the most familiar probably is John Walton, working from the 1800s to his death in 1839, when his factory was continued by his widow. Whether he was copied by his rivals or merely expressed the mood of his day, the fact remains that every cottage collector today knows the Walton style, the cheap brittle earthenware, the crude colouring with a "dry" texture, the delight in sentimental rustic subjects, domestic peace and simple faith that reflected a period of upheaval and tension. As mentioned above, for background to such figure groups as his "Rural Pastimes" he might elaborate the usual figure support into a stumpy tree with a few large oak leaves stamped out from the clay—characteristically with somewhat

V-shaped tops—arranged in groups centred with flowers, meant perhaps to be acorn cups. Half a dozen leaves may suffice for a single child figure or a fan of four leafy branches, twenty or thirty leaves, for the raven's perch behind Elijah.

Walton occasionally used formal square plinths in the earlier tradition painted to suggest marble, but the typical base is as casual and easily shaped as befitted the general trend, a tall rocky mound with a recess for a scroll at the front containing a brief, obvious title and on the back perhaps an impressed mark, WALTON. A pair of ram and ewe may each have a lamb snuggled into a recess in the mound, a homely detail that a buyer might be pleased to remember from a country childhood.

Ralph Salt made small figures from about 1820 and built a larger pottery in 1834. When he died in 1846 his son Charles continued the style into the 1860s, though not the quality of finish. The name may be found impressed on the back of a base in the Walton style, a rocky mound, slightly waisted, supporting a tree stump bocage behind the figure. Some of the odd little figures in earthenware illustrating *The Three Tours of Dr. Syntax* are by Salt, copied from Derby bone china. Other makers in the Walton style are known merely by an occasional mark. J. DALE BURSLEM mark a set of four Elements and a bust of John Wesley at the Victoria and Albert Museum, and Edge & Grocott may be mentioned, known for a few bocage groups, and Turner & Abbott.

Obadiah Sherratt is associated with grotesque bull-baiting pieces, but gradually more of his work is coming to light and suggests a go-ahead potter with a lively interest in his public. His contrasting scenes of elegance and debauchery in the pair "Teetotal" and "Ale bench" have a care for detail as well as for humour that was soon lost in this hurrying age. Sherratt's use of a conspicuous style of plinth for his wide-based figure groups suggests the showman in him. This was shaped like massively bracket-footed furniture. He was at work by 1815 and after his death in the 1840s his son and widow continued into the late 1850s.

Some collectors credit Sherratt with a crime piece of 1828, the first example of what became popular ornaments and seem to have lost none of their appeal. These, though probably unintentionally, derided the genteel cottage-shaped pastille burners of early 19th-century bone china. The crime piece was essentially a simple model of a building, usually nondescript enough but named as the scene of a crime or the home of criminal or victim. This early specimen is the red barn at Polstead and is more elaborate than most, since it includes the figures of Maria Marten and her murderer, William Corder. Stanfield Hall and Potash Farm came in 1848 in the same ghoulish mood. These are unmarked and so are most of these rough and ready wares.

Such celebrities as Nelson and Napoleon were too long popular for easy dating, but others may be placed because their renown was soon forgotten: the actor John Liston, for example, is found carrying a hat box in the character of Paul Pry, staged in 1826. Jack Crawford was the Sunderland hero of the Camperdown incident of 1797, nailing the colours to the mast, a feat long recorded by the Sunderland potters.

Sunderland, of course, was always a market for popular souvenirs of all kinds to mark the comings and goings of seamen and their families. Plaques, frog mugs, jugs with views of the famous bridge, often sparkling with spatterings of lustre, are as sure of a welcome today as when they were made. But none have retained their gaudy insouciance better than those Sunderland figures from the South Hylton and Garrison Potteries and probably from other competing firms. The occasional marked specimen is usually in somewhat coarse earthenware, its subject ranging from hero or sentimental shepherd to one of the ever-popular Seasons. Sunderland celebrity figures were as varied as Joan of Arc and Queen Victoria.

Highlanders were made at Sunderland too, but more may be associated with the Scottish potteries. Of these perhaps the best known was Portobello, acquired in 1808 by Thomas Rathbone, a go-ahead potter whose main work was among useful wares but who seems to have produced some simple bocage figures and shepherds in tartan, and many a stolid little fishwife with her creel on her shoulders. Again his rivals' lack of marks makes attribution difficult.

Rathbone was one of many who made small figure group watch stands. Set in a hole in the centre of such a group a watch would serve as a bedside clock. In the nonsensical way of these things some Victorians preferred these groups set around useless painted watch faces; maybe they did not have to rise betimes. Rathbone depended on the gaudy brightness of a few underglaze colours to sell his cheaper "dabbities": William Baird in 1898 recorded the success of Portobello's "classic and rustic figures, male and female, as fishwives, soldiers, sailors and shepherds for mantel-piece ornaments". These, he noted, were "sent in carts and retailed in all parts among the country people".

Rathbone had to close for a time in the depression of the late 1830s and never really recovered before ceasing in the 1850s. But many an enthusiast today regards that as the very period when many potters were beginning their phenomenally successful run of the chimney ornaments known now as flat-backs. These are ornaments of such specialized purpose that at any rate by the 1840s or 1850s neither potter nor purchaser saw any need to worry about the plain backs pressed against the chimney breast. One way and another potters were able to price these figures cheaply enough to sell in quantities that might seem to leave little enough opportunity for the ill-coloured fakes all-too-prevalent today.

Many collectors specialize in these companionable small figures—and not so small too, for some were made in a range of sizes and priced in pennies or shillings accordingly. All, of course, vary from piece to piece as regards clarity of outline and general finish, for their moulds soon became worn and only the best were worth meticulous brushwork.

This was no sudden outburst. As shown above, souvenir figures of royalty and other celebrities had been in vogue throughout the early 19th century. Queen Caroline was modelled as a result of public sympathy during her trial of 1820. William IV is noted with and without Queen Adelaide. Celebrities ranged from John Wilkes with his support for "the rights of the people" to Nelson, General Sir John Moore (d. 1809) and more than a dozen different versions of John Wesley. Even Grace Darling's exploit of

1838 had its small cottage-and-lighthouse model with tiny figures of the heroine and her father in their boat.

Flat-back versions of royalty appear to have begun no earlier than 1840, however, when Victoria married Albert, beginning a remarkable record of the family. It is possible to trace the progress of the children, for example, from the baby Princess Royal with her parents, and the royal children at play and even asleep, watched by a guardian angel, to the Princess Royal and her husband, Frederick William of Prussia, when they married in 1857 and when he became Crown Prince in 1861. The Prince of Wales too may be found through childhood and youth, from kilt and Shetland pony to flowered waistcoats and splendid horse, through his engagement and marriage and that of his brother Alfred. Associated figures include, of course, Princess Alexandra of Denmark and "Princess May" of Teck, the latter recorded delightfully in 1891.

Victoria herself is found in many poses, including Crimean War groups when she is flanked by the King of Sardinia and Napoleon III. The 1870 Jubilee figure continued the tradition, but by then the medium was losing its freshness and few late figures are remarkable. General Gordon was modelled, camel-mounted, as late as the 1880s and Gladstone in the 1890s. Early figures include Wellington ("Up guards and at them"), the Earl of Shaftesbury with a ragged-school boy, Richard Cobden with a wheatsheaf, Robert Peel, even the Irish Nationalist, William Smith O'Brien, paired with his loyal wife and wearing the manacles that recorded his life-transportation to Australia. The collector has to recall the No Popery outburst of the early 1850s to understand the figures of Latimer and Ridley and of Cranmer among the burning faggots, but many other figures are easily placed. Robert Burns was popular, paired in the later issues with his Highland Mary, and Sir Walter Scott with tartan plaid and trim pink trousers. A figure entitled "Bloomers" commemorates dress-reformer Amelia Bloomer, and for contrast there is Will Watch the smuggler, commemorating the success of the play *Will Watch and his Black-eyed Sue*, and, in the many reproductions now about, a potential danger to tyro collectors today.

These are but a few of the many who can be identified, but collectors find many more figures that are anonymous —brave Highlanders, children with their pets, sentimental lovers. All suggest the day-to-day characters that a chance purchaser at the time could identify with his own circumscribed existence, although in the manner of their period every group of harvesters had to be Ruth and Naomi, every pair of soldiers became fraternizing allies.

Collectors trace the gradual reduction of the out-jutting detail that contributed to the cost of early pieces. At the same time they note the colour change. By the 1850s the brilliant glossy whiteness of the ware no longer required the colours that had masked the blemishes in earlier cheap figures. Alike in dusky cottage and much-curtained, fade-defying, north-facing parlour the pairs of figures were seen most clearly when this startling whiteness was merely touched with lines of gold and black and colour. Gold especially is welcome on figures of this kind and became an economic proposition from 1853 when a bright liquid gold was invented by William Cornelius. So it is left to us today to mourn the loss of the superb blue that dominated the early colouring.

Subsidiary and altogether less brilliant colour painted over the glaze has tended to flake—light red or orange for cloaks and Garibaldi's shirt—green for trimmings, with ermine strictly for royalty, black for shoes, though Jenny Lind as Maria in *The Daughter of the Regiment* (about 1847) might have red for her little button boots. To the specialist these colour details are, as it were, part of the code that identified a politician by his frock coat, a cleric by his pulpit, an author or poet by his book, a soldier by accompanying guns and shot, a sailor by an anchor. These clues may well prove necessary today for by no means all figures are named and few faces show any attempt at characterization. Indeed in contrast to the hearty, earthy quality of the century's early years the chimney figures tended gradually to acquire a glossy unreality often scarcely less vapid than their most frequent companion on the mantelshelf, the comforter dog.

Chapter Nine

COPPER LUSTRE

O F all cottage ceramic wares copper lustre is the favourite, the most evocative or provocative according to one's mood of romantic speculation or practical enquiry. Even the name is misleading. What every collector wants is lustre ware in the range of glowing mellow tones, warmer than brass, brighter than copper, derived in fact from minute quantities of gold. Its indefinable charm is not made any the more explicable by the fact that one frequently finds, as the basis for its colour, thin washes in tones of pinkish-purple applied upon wares of reddish-brown.

Iridescent lustre was applied to pottery more than a thousand years ago in Mesopotamia, in North Persia from the 12th and 13th centuries, and most splendidly in the Valencia area of Spain from the 14th century. But the Hispano-Moresque style of decorating in lustre upon tin-enamelled earthenware—developed also in Italy from the late 15th century—was remote in style and purpose from the homely English product. Here, it appears, the aim always has been to catch the light gleam of just-polished metal in vessels that defied the atmospheric challenges of steamy kitchen or shuttered parlour. "Silver" lustre pieces, entirely covered with the lustre derived from platinum, might be shaped and ornamented to suggest the rich man's silver plate but the potter seldom saw much sense in any laborious imitation of vessels in either gold or copper and made instead a range of useful wares in a variety of style and ornament that are entirely distinctive as well as of lasting delight.

Like so much in the story of everyday English ceramics, the beginnings may be traced to the late 18th century. Go-ahead potters were then thankfully abandoning the

91

various problems involved in making tin-enamelled delft ware, faience, white salt-glazed stoneware and clumsy slip ware. Instead, for table use, they concentrated upon the improved cream-coloured earthenwares that at last were adequately meeting the workaday need for clean, light, serviceable vessels. For kitchenware the public still turned to the brown-ware potters, making brown salt-glazed stoneware, but found also the beginnings of another highly successful phase as coarse earthenwares were covered with a stronger glaze stained manganese-brown evolved around 1790 by the Rockingham pottery and still known as rockingham glaze.

John William Hancock, an enameller who worked for Josiah Spode at Stoke, claimed that he produced "gold, silver and steel lustre at Spode's factory in 1789". Various other experiments have been recorded and it seems probable that an important contribution to the styles of lustre here under review came from Dr. Fothergill to Josiah Wedgwood not long before the latter's death in 1796. At all events, the great period for the ware was the first half of the 19th century—for jugs, mugs, goblets, tea-ware, for peppers, salts and mustard pots, bowls, barbers' dishes, ewers and washbasins, even the occasional tea caddy as well as purely ornamental work ranging from mantelshelf figures of men and animals to lustre-framed texts for hanging on the wall. Probably almost every pottery district active in the early 19th century produced some of this ware, from Bristol to Newcastle, from Middlesbrough to Liverpool, from Scotland to Yorkshire and Staffordshire.

The desirable piece feels light in the hands, its surface lustrously smooth, unpitted, uncrazed, such details as handle or spout shapely and well finished, its rim usually thin and in consequence showing bare of lustre where it has caught the rub of wear. Some early potters applied their tenuous film of gold to the glazed cream-coloured earthenware and caught a gleam bright as a new guinea piece. But that, comparatively, was luxury ware: the more substantial the film of gold the brighter but less iridescent the gleam. In some of the brightest the metallic oxide was in fact obtained from gold guineas, although gold of lower

19. Among earthenware ornaments, cows are so popular that they have been reproduced widely but genuine cow milk jugs may still be found occasionally, copied from a silver model introduced by John Schüppe in the 1750s. The intention was that the vessel could be filled by a lidded aperture in the back and poured through the open "lowing" mouth. They have been made in all manner of wares from white and brown stonewares to pearl ware, stone china and even bone china. Figure ornaments of the 18th century were mainly intended for a middle-class public able to recognize such pieces as the pearl ware busts above. These have the typical deep plinths of the Leeds Pottery and are emblematic of Water and Air. Water has green weed in her hair and a dolphin head in her cloak; Air has an eagle's skin across his shoulders. They are 6½ inches tall and date to about 1790.

20a. Chimney ornaments in Staffordshire earthenware. This lion and unicorn are set against branches of oak leaves in the stylized manner introduced by earthenware potters seeking to reproduce the flowered arbours or bocages popular in fine porcelain. This attractive pair were made as souvenirs for George IV's coronation, 1821.

20b. In contrast to the cheap little souvenirs the previous century found a ready market for the realistic animal modelling of Whieldon, Wood and others. This well-observed figure of a fox standing over a dead cock has been noted too in Whieldon colouring, but here is an uncoloured Leeds piece of about 1790.

carat, alloyed with copper, gave the ware a pleasanter, warmer tone. The Cambrian Pottery, Swansea, for example, used a fine hard earthenware known as opaque china and as late as 1807 their London warehouse was advertising "ware ornamented with an entire new Golden Lustre".

As war conditions made it difficult and expensive for potters to obtain gold, however, those making lustre for a high-quality market tended to concentrate instead on the silver effects achieved with the newly developed metal platinum. Some were in direct imitation of silver and Sheffield plate and some in the delicate effects of pattern now classed as silver resist. A certain amount of gold resist pattern was produced also, on cream or white glazed vessels.

The cottage copper lustre ware now most widely collected, however, was evolved when by skilful chemistry an extremely thin film of gold was applied to the homelier brown-glazed earthenware. Sometimes one finds the vessel formed entirely of such ware, sometimes the brown covers a core of whiter ware and sometimes the white is introduced either to line a vessel on the inside or to band it on the outside as a background to coloured ornament. In the early 1820s highly polished red stoneware was found an effective base, fired at an intense heat to render it strong and impervious to liquids without glaze. Dr. Simeon Shaw in *The Chemistry of Pottery*, 1828, named John Hancock, John Gardner and William Henning as responsible in 1823 for introducing lustre applied directly to a reddish-brown clay, specially prepared, rich in colour and mirror smooth.

The basic method of the lustre potter was to dissolve his metal in a mixture of hydrochloric and nitric acids. This solution was added to balsam of sulphur and oil of turpentine, thinned with oil of lavender. With the metal held in suspension the mixture was brush painted upon the ware— more thinly and evenly than was possible by dipping. Gentle firing in a muffle kiln for 8 to 12 hours left the reduced metal entirely covering the surface, brilliant without burnishing, entirely smooth, but so thin that its edge defies detection by the finger tip and often it shows a diffractive "soap bubble" iridescence.

Textbooks of the period such as A. Ure's *Dictionary of*

Arts, Manufactures and Mines indicate that some tin oxide was added to the gold. "If the lustre is too light or pale, more gold must be added, and if it have not a sufficient violet or purple tint, more tin must be used." Fothergill's important contribution to the development of this ware was his suggestion that a less expensive lustre could be obtained from the metallic substance known as purple of cassius. The exotic sounding colour evolved by a 17th-century German physician was produced by the action of tin chloride on gold chloride. This precipitate required more tin than gold and in direct light a wash of the solution appears purple upon the brown earthenware. When held at a slant to the light, however, it reveals a lustrous fire. On examination most of the early 19th-century copper lustre found today proves to hold this underlying purple tone although it may require close scrutiny to detect it. A late piece may show traces of a cheaper lack-lustre mauve under the lustre wash.

In comparable silver lustring upon dark brown earthenware a single coating of the platinum solution produced a steely tone and a second coating a more silvery brilliance and it appears probable that much cheap-selling copper lustre acquired its indescribable hue from a double coating of this purple of cassius or a similar preparation then implied by the name gold-purple. The firm of Allerton, making lustre from its foundation in 1831, reported to J. F. Blacker as late as about 1910 that gold lustre "or copper as it is sometimes called" was far cheaper than silver (platinum) lustre to produce and was still in considerable demand at home and abroad. The Wedgwood firm was making lustre wares by 1805 including their moonlight lustre deploying the purple tones in effects of marbling.

For most collectors the lovely coppery tone of the metallic lustre is pleasure enough, its sparkle often enhanced by horizontal ribbing—on the lower body of a jug for example —or the twists of a mug handle in lamprey form. Often a jug or bowl or goblet has three or more lines of beading around the body, a detail used more extensively on lustres imitating Sheffield plate. In copper lustre I have noted rim beading only on recent work, sometimes in association with a surface lightly moulded to suggest hammering, a detail

94

unlikely to appeal to the early 19th-century lustre potter who, even if seeking to imitate beaten copper, would look to smooth planishing as the criterion.

Usually, however, the potter introduced additional ornament. Collectors can find quite a range of different styles but little to suggest any chronological sequence. Around the turn of the century a number of potters were turning again to the early form of decoration known as sprigging, shaping ornamental motifs in small metal moulds and attaching them to the ware. White reliefs in classical style are associated especially with Wedgwood's soft-toned jaspers but are to be found too in the brilliant setting of copper lustre. Robert Wilson of Hanley was among the potters who developed this old technique, using sprigs of pictorial groups completely surrounded by the wash of lustre. Some classical figures in this style on tea-ware are ascribed to John Shorthose, Hanley (1783–1826). An obvious simplification consisted of a band of glazed white around a vessel. This was of better quality than the flawy white often found lining the lower part of a jug but nonetheless tends to show the fine cracks known as crazing that indicate earthenware and glaze imperfectly matched in their response to changes of atmosphere. I have never seen crazing in the copper lustre itself: its lustrous smoothness is one of its most endearing traits and the eventual deterioration to gritty, pimply surface blemishes an obvious reason for the ware's eclipse.

This band of white-glazed ware could be ornamented by simple hand painting in colours or, as often, in the gold-purple which appears pinkish-mauve at its palest and copper-toned where applied more substantially. Some of these simple freehand flowers and tendrils are particularly attractive. Sometimes, apparently, paper stencils were used, producing patterns in white against a lustre ground. The well-known potter John Davenport of Longport in about 1806 obtained a reverse effect by coating stencil-covered ware with wax. When the paper was removed the background was still protected by the wax against the subsequent applications of the lustre and when the wax was removed the lustre pattern could be fixed by firing.

The more familiar resist method of lustre ornament

evolved in about 1810 required the hand painting of the design upon the glazed surface in a resist material such as pulverized china clay moistened with glycerine or honey. The result was a pattern in white or colour against a background of lustre and this usually covered the whole jug, loving cup or other treasured vessel. But here again the process was more fully developed in silver lustre wares.

On the shining copper surface even the band of white or cream glaze may seem an unnecessary intrusion. From the late 1820s an alternative was a ground colour. This was applied over the white by the ground-laying process introduced in 1826 by Henry Daniell of Shelton. It required greater kiln heat than the lustre and often it is possible to see where the subsequent wash of lustre has been brushed over the edge of the colour—which is most usually buff, blue, yellow, apricot, pink or a heavy bluish or yellowish-green. Thomas Barlow of Longton impressed a *B* on some lustred jugs with flower patterns on bands of brilliant yellow.

Sometimes this colour was applied carefully around flowers and other simple ornament left in the white, a method simplified when the pattern was moulded in low relief in the course of shaping the vessel.

Enoch Wood and Elijah Mayer were among the first to cast the reliefs in this way from the early 1820s. Such reliefs tended to lose their clear-cut edges and often the lustre was too quickly applied around them for perfect definition. From the general style of the work thus ornamented it is obvious that this was, on the whole, a later development than the flat painted band ornament. Similar ornament is found on homely brown ware of mid- or late-Victorian days, the motifs sometimes including an individual name and date—peasant art at its most endearing

The extreme of relief shaping, of course, is found in the occasional character jug or mug which is difficult to date. Admiral Rodney had been an obvious favourite with seamen from as early as his French victory in 1782. The lustred mug shaped as his head is a museum rarity but an occasional jug is found with mask spout, the head in an admiral's hat still proving acceptable several decades after Derby first issued its popular Rodney vessels.

21a. Mid-19th-century chimney ornaments. These Victorian flat-backs are typical of great numbers of topical figures. *Left:* Victor Emmanuel, king of Sardinia, an ally of Britain in the Crimean War who visited the country in 1855; he became king of Italy in 1861. Beside him is Lord Raglan who commanded the British Army in the Crimea until his death in 1855. *Right:* Miss Nightingale with a dashing army officer, one of three models commemorating her work made in 1855.

21b. Slipware, also of the mid-19th century, made by G. Fishley of Fremington, Devon. These ornaments are in red earthenware with modelled decoration in red, white and dark brown. The central covered goblet is flanked by two watch-stands with masks, birds pecking grapes and tiny foreground figures including Napoleon.

22. Gleaming copper lustre ware. *Top left:* the putti and chariot design is in white low relief, mould-shaped separately and sprigged on to the jug surface. *Top right:* the band of white is hand painted in colours and purple lustre. *Centre:* two goblets, one with lustre-covered moulded figures on a green ground and one with a simple resist pattern against a purple of cassius ground. *Bottom left:* cup and saucer with sprigged ornament made by John Shorthose, Hanley (at work 1783–1826). *Bottom right:* flowers moulded and painted against a band of blue.

Most delightful of all, perhaps, are some of the wholly copper-lustred figure ornaments, though these are sadly rare today. The most notable figure maker who included lustres in his palette was Enoch Wood of Burslem. The mark *Wood & Caldwell* indicates a partnership dating 1790–1818. Alternative treatment by this firm included all-silver (platinum) lustre and painting in lustre and colour. Animals are familiar, with dabs and spots of copper lustre. These include cow cream jugs and comforter dogs and equally stiff little cats made for mid-Victorian mantelshelves and to furbish the summer hearth. But occasionally a far finer animal is found such as the all-copper-brown bull in Sunderland Museum thought to have been made by the firm of Dawson & Co., Low Ford.

Many collectors of copper lustre wares widen their field by including the wares known as Sunderland. The tin-gold lustre such as purple of cassius is easily recognized when applied upon glazed white or cream-coloured earthenware and is the basis of this range of wares. It is interesting to note that to earlier generations "Sunderland ware" was the brown-glazed ware. On the light-toned ware the pink or purple carries the same copper-toned lustre and often is rimmed with the more intense deep copper. It is of course a product of all the regions that catered for a popular market—Bristol, Newcastle, Liverpool, Staffordshire as well as Sunderland.

Sunderland was of all cheap ornament the brightest and most forthright and calculated to take the fancy of seamen and factory folk looking for souvenirs to give their families or to display as mementoes of home. The tone at its lightest is pale rose but on the rim of a jug or the frame of a wall text it may show its richest coppery fire. Lacking the earthy brown background an economically thin wash of colour might be expected to produce patchy results when brush-applied and it seems probable that this prompted the deliberate mottlings characteristic of the ware—a poor man's substitute for the intricacies of lustre-resists. The most sparing use of colour became permissible when unevenness was exaggerated into a haphazard pattern by spattering with oil applied as tiny droplets by being blown

7

through a tube covered with fine muslin. As the lustre was fired in the muffle kiln the oil expanded as small bubbles which burst in irregular patterns.

The Sunderland Museum has surveyed the lustres produced by local potteries including this spattered effect in a colour range classed by collectors as pink, purple, gold or ruby. Dinner services were made and tea-sets, jugs, mugs, bowls and such ornamental pieces as plaques, tiles and mantelshelf figures and animals. Often the main ornament is a transfer-printed view of the Wear Bridge and printed detail may give a clue to the date. Much of this pink ware was marked, but in its full copper tone on brown ware the lustre made in large quantities by most of these Wearside firms very rarely bears a mark. Exactly attributed pieces in this museum include many from the Garrison Pottery, ranging from copper and silver lustre jugs commemorating Queen Victoria's marriage in 1840 to a lustre-ornamented mantelshelf watch stand, its figures flanking a grandfather clock: this is marked Dixon Austin & Co. so that it can be dated to 1820–26, well before the Victorian chimney ornament era.

Pink and copper tones of lustre could add particularly effective touches of colour and brightness to rims and details of moulded or painted ornament and lustre ware of this kind is widely collected. Silver resist lustre was always a good-quality product but when copper or pink lustre was introduced on fine wares it appears that it was usually sanctioned only as small touches of subsidiary detail. The familiar strawberry pattern, for example, found on marked tea services from both Minton and New Hall, 1820–30, has most delicate touches of pink lustre among the berries and leaves. Hard fired earthenwares such as those known as opaque china were used, as they were for the gold resist on creamy earthenware or white bone china that is a rare variant of the sought-after, much copied silver resist.

There was also some attempt to apply transfer-printed patterns in lustre, Peter Warburton of New Hall patenting a method in 1810. This was a variant of the familiar bat printing which conveyed the design from the engraved copper plate to the ware in an oil mixture upon a bat or pad made of glue and isinglass. The metal lustre in powder form was spread upon the ware, adhering to the oil impression, to be fixed by gentle kiln firing. Other potters associated with lustre ware of the more costly types thought worthy of record included John Shorthose of Hanley, John Aynsley of Lane End, Bailey & Batkin of Longton, Lakin & Poole of Hanley, J. F. Wileman of Longton. Josiah Wedgwood with moonlight lustre, the Leeds Pottery and Thomas Minton of Stoke were notable for brilliant work.

A collection of tea-ware, jugs and mugs lightly touched with lustre can cover some of the best useful wares of this period. In speedy hand painting and in the laborious detail of transfer-print the collector finds references to current political excitement, recognition of naval and military heroes, crude commemoration of sporting events, caricature disparagement of such obvious enemies as Bonaparte. There are traces of wry humour, too, as well as the more usual run of sentimental pictures and the doggerel verse that is some collectors' particular delight.

Variation in ornament is endless. Sometimes the surface is moulded in light relief in an all-over design suggesting the current diamond-cutting on jugs of glass as a background to lustre-touched flowers. Sometimes the whole ornament is hand painted in the lustrous purple of cassius with primitive views of buildings and trees: one in the Stoke City Museum is named and dated 1815 and similar ornament may be found on teapots and other tea-ware associated with some of the Sunderland potteries.

J. F. Blacker more than fifty years ago warned collectors against the lustre wares then being distributed by the Staffordshire potters to the antique shops of the world and today a disappointingly large proportion of the pieces found prove to be inferior work. The band of white or colour may be free of disfiguring crazing on this late work but the metallic surface lacks the earlier flawless sheen, being applied apparently over an imperfect brown ground and further flawed by pittings and bubbles. The ware itself is heavy, the lustre dark although sometimes applied over a wash of a more golden brown or orange tone. An orange tone rather than the earlier rose pink has been noted in the lustre produced by the Sunderland Ball's Pottery established

1857 which added to our confusion by lustre-decorating ornament printed by transfer from copper plates acquired from earlier potteries, sometimes incorporating their names.

A teapot is especially desirable in copper lustre. Occasionally an early specimen is found with the high upswept collar and well-proportioned body of the Regency: this may be painted in purple lustre. Some only a little later have square-oblong bodies and still shapely but higher lids. But more have the high lid, wide sloping shoulder and sagging, high-waisted body of the 1840s–50s—a gem nevertheless when the surface is copper lustre, perhaps painted with sprays of flowers.

Bowls were often sold in sets of twelve but for collecting in quantity to set out upon the shelf mugs may prove a better proposition. They should begin with a light-in-the-hands, wide, low vessel, virtually as wide as it is high and with no shaping save for a well-curved handle and no ornament save a band of flowers, perhaps, on a white glazed ground. Other designs may show somewhat flaring rim and foot rim, followed by the waisted outline in a concave curve from the rim to the base which often has, as it were, a second base exaggerating the curve. Some of these have indeterminately knobbed handles which tend to lack the shapely conventional curve of earlier work. This concave outline is associated with much copper lustre probably of the 1830s–40s— sugar bowls, goblets, spill vases.

Some of the most attractive stemmed goblets are in the bucket bowl outline associated with drinking glasses of Regency days. Others, later, have bowls in ogee curves with the more pronounced bas-relief ornament of their period. Another characteristic outline found in lustre goblets, salt cellars, sugar bowls and the like, is the early Victorian high-waisted curve ending in a flat, projecting base-rim— often beaded—above stem and foot rim.

Copper lustre jugs may vary in size from $2\frac{1}{2}$-gallon capacity to $2\frac{1}{2}$ inches in height. An early lustre-touched specimen may be in the so-called Liverpool shape of around 1800, the body more or less a barrel with a slightly wider base-rim to balance a high, wide spout and broad handle. More are found in perhaps the best shape ever devised for jugs with a well-pointed spout projecting from a short, vertical, straight-topped rim above a rounded, gently tapering body that ends in a low, small-diameter base-rim. Here the handle is the well-scrolled, square-shouldered work of the 1800s, often with a vertical grip ending in a double-C curve before it meets the body. The style is associated with a widespread development of interest in jug ornament in low relief such as men and animals in genre scenes, patriotic figures of Britannia and current heroes and simple pastoral subjects: here lustre appears as an alternative to other cheap gaiety such as the high-temperature colour work known as Pratt ware.

The rim soon tended to widen and dip, the spout to rise and increase in importance; the whole style lost its neat formality. More lustre jugs are found with very large rounded spouts and deep rims. Many of these were high-shouldered still with tapering bodies, the spout being a well-made detail often with a decorative petal edge where it meets the body, sometimes a mask outline. In some specimens the high, wide spout is set in a widely everted, wavy edged rim almost as wide as the rounded body—a friendly, generous-looking jug usually with a magnificent high-scrolling handle.

Gradually the style became taller and thinner with a longer narrower neck. The body might still be in inverted pear shape but on a wide foot-rim and all too soon the design further deteriorated with a sagging body that reached its maximum circumference only a little above the foot-rim. The low wide-mouthed cream pitcher was usually lustred throughout its interior but the serving jug with a deep narrow-diameter rim was lustred inside only to the bottom of the rim, the lower interior showing somewhat flawy white. By the 1860s many jugs were more or less straight with small lip and dull handle so that collectors look elsewhere for attractive pieces—to the squat little cream pitcher, perhaps. This may be wide-spouted on a silversmith's panelled body, sometimes with small feet in the Regency manner. Or it may be small-rimmed on a full round body, another neat, early outline, soon followed by all the less coherent shapes of early and mid-Victorian imagination.

Chapter Ten

ONCE upon a time a rich Chinese mandarin lived in a magnificent pagoda beside a river. His beautiful daughter Koong-Shee was affianced to a rich merchant Ta-Jin, but she lost her heart instead to her father's secretary Chang. When her father found out he dismissed Chang and confined his daughter to a room in the pagoda overlooking the willow-fringed river. One day she received a letter from Chang floating in a tiny boat of coconut shell. In despair of ever marrying her he threatened suicide but she answered him with the message: "The fruit you prize must be gathered when the willow catkins dance on the boughs." Chang caught her meaning and watched for the culmination of the wedding preparations and in the confused excitement of the ceremonies entered the pagoda and fled with Koong-Shee over the little bridge beneath the willow trees, seeking refuge in the island house beyond. The mandarin angrily pursued them, threatening to have them beaten to death, but just as capture seemed inevitable the young lovers were transformed into turtle doves and flew away to happiness.

So runs the story of the pattern that first enchanted Englishmen in the sentimental days of the late 18th century and has been presented ever since in the wares known and loved throughout the world as Staffordshire blue. Occasionally the maker and the date of a piece of willow pattern may be determined. The patterns varied in detail but now most usually present the complete scene showing the pagoda among the pine and willow trees, the three figures upon the bridge—Koong-Shee with her virgin's distaff, her lover Chang with her jewel box dowry and the mandarin with his whip—and showing also the rejected Ta-Jin approaching in his boat and the blue birds flying away to happiness. No other pattern ever has so successfully caught the public's imagination with its combination of matter-of-fact detail and happy fantasy. None has remained so dateless.

To the collector any piece of old blue willow is worth more than a passing glance, whether it is an individual sauceboat, jug or pickle plate or a huge meat platter or soup tureen from a massive Regency dinner service. Some pieces are marked on the back with their potters' names or initials. From these others may be identified and sometimes dated—by their patterns of story and border, by the manner of their reproduction, by the tones of their blues and of the underlying ware or by the quality and texture of their glaze. Much of what may be deduced from such scrutiny is valuable too in assessing other pieces of Staffordshire blue.

To the collector with a flair for finding treasure among old junk, a collection of Staffordshire blue in a single theme suggests endless possibilities and the most delightful results upon the cottage plate-racks over the dresser. The patterns may be willow or "picturesque views" or even comical scenes from the Rowlandson drawings of "Dr. Syntax": it is left to the shrewd collector to identify the valuable early piece among the later more hackneyed and stereotyped. The rare occasional find may be an identifiable American view, for example, reproduced from a drawing made on the spot by an English artist sent for the purpose by an enterprising English exporter.

Blue willow remains the outstanding phenomenon, however, for it was created at the beginning of the whole fascinating story and seems likely to outlive all rivals. The basis, of course, was the fact that English potters like the Chinese before them found blue to be almost the only colour that could be applied to wares under the glaze, unaffected by the heat required to fire the glaze and therefore preserved by this glaze from knife wear and acid stains and from all the atmospheric hazards of smoky, steamy kitchens.

Through the 18th century innumerable patterns were hand-painted in blue upon English wares inspired by Chinese originals. But from the late 18th century onwards the need was for output in good-looking everyday wares on a scale that could meet the demands of a vast new public.

Wedgwood's pearl ware and other improved earthenwares were strong and clean but most potters were conscious of surface blemishes that needed the disguise of all-over patterns and this was England's particular triumph. The slipshod decoration that resulted from hand-painting at commercially economic speed may be welcomed as quaint today but at the time the public was as delighted as the potter to encounter elaborate, meticulously detailed decoration applied to the ware by methods within the scope of any woman-and-child team in the factory workshop.

This was transfer-printing. A specialist engraver cut a suitable pattern upon a copper plate and from this it was printed upon paper in a pigment appropriate to the earthenware, and printed again and again so that the potter had enough transfer papers to put identical borders on every piece of many a table service. Once dry these papers were easy to handle—are easy, for the process is still universal. The child cut the transfer papers roughly to the shapes required and the woman fitted them, face downward, upon the ware which was in the once-fired, unglazed porous state known as biscuit. In a circular border it is usually possible to see where the pattern is joined but a conspicuous break in the pattern suggests cheap work. Firing in the kiln fixed the pattern and there was the ware ready for glazing. Details have changed but the principle of this method is still at the root of almost all our ornament on useful wares to this day.

Its origins may be traced in fascinating detail to as early as the mid-18th century as an adaptation of the customary method of printing pictures from engraved copper plates. But here it is enough to say that by 1780 Thomas Turner of the Caughley factory in Shropshire had succeeded in transfer-printing in blue underglaze on cream ware and then more successfully on pearl ware and the first willow pattern had been engraved on copper plates still in existence. Turner was not the originator of transfer-printing on ceramics but must be credited with the experimental advances upon earthenware and with the willow design itself which owes little to any known Chinese original.

Blue willow only became widely available, however—

and to most households the first-ever decorated table ware —when its potential was appreciated by Josiah Spode (1733–97). With two craftsmen from Caughley he launched it in the Potteries, evolving a clear hard glaze and by 1785 was making his own version of the willow pattern. Soon the whole great region of the English Potteries was prospering with him. When Spode died he was succeeded by his son working in association with W. Copeland. From 1827 a son of each family continued the firm and from 1829 W. T. Copeland was left as sole proprietor so that the firm's later Staffordshire blue carries Copeland marks (Copeland & Garrett between 1833 and 1847).

John Davenport issued willow from 1793 to 1830 including magnificent services richly gilded on rims and handles. Wedgwood made blue willow from 1795, and some printed in black from about 1830. Further afield the same pattern may be found coming from Swansea and from Leeds. Spode's earliest design is interesting. By later standards the early engravers cut too deep, the paper transferred too much colour and early attempts at fine detail such as cross-hatching appeared smudgy on the imperfect biscuit ware. Nevertheless the mandarin's pagoda with its water and trees is full of dark but lively detail, with two pigtailed figures struggling in front—Chang presumably trying to escape the mandarin's fury while Koong-Shee goes ahead over the bridge, Ta-Jin's boat founders in the foreground and only the birds are missing to supply the happy ending.

I suppose collectors always tend to look first at those figures on the bridge—two in some early pieces by Liverpool's Herculaneum Pottery and in some by Caughley too where the birds quickly acquired their traditional pose and a tall pine tree dominated the characteristic three-pillared pagoda. Some collectors prefer to regard this as an apple tree and indeed for that period the whole arboreal setting of the willow pattern is remarkably representational —formalistic rather than lifelike, in fact, in the practical mood of the Walton bocage (Chapter Eight). The straightforward topographical views that followed were taken mainly from book illustrations and when an original engraving comes to light it is possible to realize what skill

was required of the potter's engraver to present an acceptable, entirely understandable précis of the painstakingly
delicate original. In defiance of the inevitable hard outlines on
the earthenware, Wedgwood issued some in what is known
as flown blue with slight intentional blurring but some collectors like this as little as an out-of-focus photograph.

Leeds and Swansea appear to have issued very similar
willow patterns in the early style with two figures on the
bridge and the third emerging from the pagoda: this has
the three pillars but lacks some of the later foreground
details including the zigzag fence that soon became a
decorative detail for filling the bare space at the bottom of
the scene. Davenport, with two figures on the bridge and a
simple little pagoda, might include the fence but instead
of flying birds put a couple of plump ducks swimming in
the foreground water. Later of course, like Spode, Minton
and many others, he conformed with the usual pattern of
three figures on the bridge, two birds in flight above.

Sometimes in the later blue willows a firm may be distinguished by the numbers of "apples" on the dominant tree,
thirty-two being most usual while some such as Wedgwood
might show thirty-five or more and Benjamin Adams as
many as fifty. By 1830 there were nearly 200 makers of
this pattern but it had become just a routine line and few
marked it with the small motifs and initials that every
collector hopes for when looking under any piece of ware.
Potters whose willow may be identified by marks include
J. & G. Rogers of Burslem (1802–42); J. E. Baddeley;
J. & R. Clews (1818–29); L. W. Dillwyn of Swansea;
Hicks, Meigh & Johnson (1822–36).

The collector finds other very similar patterns with a
strongly Chinese theme. Spode himself, for example, was
issuing his Temple pattern by 1815 with a pagoda on the
left and a bridge with two small figures on the right and he
and other potters produced other variants. Some such as
his Gothic Castle show an interesting interweaving of
Oriental and European notions. This pattern expresses in a
curiously interesting manner the period's change of
emphasis from fantasy to fact. Some Spode blue patterns
retain the romantic pastoral mood of the late 18th century

such as his Milkmaid, his Italian Tiber and Lucarno patterns. Benjamin Adams reproduced the idyllic scenes of Claude Lorrain. But even in Spode's superbly engraved Caramania series, with its faraway Asia Minor themes taken from a book published in 1802, he shows the insistence on more recognizable topographical views by a more informed public newly interested in sightseeing.

At the same time the technical processes improved. The white-surfaced earthenware known as pearl ware might be replaced by smoother, harder-surfaced stone china. By about 1810 this meant clearer reproduction of fine detail which was then engraved in both line and stipple. Until the 1830s it was always of course basically a monochrome process but engraved in varying depths that allowed for some variation in tint. This meant great exactitude in preparing colour of the right consistency and in manufacturing paper fine enough to take such printing, a detail that the Clews firm acknowledged in 1820 to have produced "astonishing improvement in printing, both on china and earthenware, more particularly the latter".

From about 1815 to 1840, then, this Staffordshire printed ware was technically superb. After 1828 underglaze transfer-printing could be carried out in red, green, black and other colours. Also more work was in printed outlines hand-coloured over the glaze. The greatest era of Staffordshire blue was drawing to a close.

Those who look first at the subjects of their ornament very occasionally find them identical on wares by different potters, their source a specialist engraver supplying transfer prints to the pottery trade. Thomas Minton was probably the first to specialize in this way. John Aynsley was another source between 1802 and 1826: his name may be found on an occasional print. The firms of Stevenson & Williams, E. Wood and J. & R. Clews are among those who may confuse the collector in this way. Ordinary shameless copying, of course, from books, pictures, even directly from each other, was universal and merciless. It was controlled only to a very limited extent by the Registration of Designs Act with its familiar diamond-shaped marks occasionally found on ceramics made between 1842 and 1883.

For a long time it was thought that each firm had its own exclusive borders but here too it is possible to find duplicates, probably due again to specialist transfer suppliers. These borders are a delight, worth studying in themselves, from the tiny vignettes in some by Spode and Jackson to the seaweeds of the Ridgway firm, the shells and grapevines of E. Wood & Sons, the acorns and oak leaves of Ralph Stevenson, American eagles of Joseph Stubbs and ambitious "Triumphal Car" by J. & M. P. Bell of Glasgow. Nearly all, as alternatives, might use rich borders of flowers such as the passion flower of both William Adams and J. & R. Clews. Only a few such as Spode related the border to the central theme, although blue willow itself was usually framed in complex borders taken from porcelain decoration and remotely adapted from the close diapers of Oriental brocade design. Some by Spode include delightfully exotic butterflies.

One of the delights of this Staffordshire blue is the prodigality of its ornament and the cheaper the basic earthenware the more it needed its flaws concealed. A single vessel would have a transfer-printed pattern applied to each face within abundant borders and every print would be different. Borders and themes kept a service together and the collector often finds that the potter has included the titles of his series and the individual subject even when omitting his own name or cryptic mark.

Most popular series probably were the English views. Castles, churches, country houses, all the tourist attractions of luscious, leafy, high summer England were bought in vast quantities by people powerless to fight their destruction by factory baron and speculative builder. Andrew Stevenson was issuing these views from about 1812, Ralph his brother from about 1816 as well as similar series such as British lakes. By then their rivals entering this field included Ralph Hall, William Adams (with over a hundred different scenes), J. & R. Clews and E. Wood & Sons, followed from the 1830s by such important contributors as T. Mayer.

In the same manner Hall and the Clews firm, for example, produced Select Views, Pictorial Views and from the Clews firm even Zoological Garden Views while William Adams of Stoke issued a series in a deep rich blue of fifteen London

Views and more came from E. Wood from about 1819. The brothers Clews, working 1819–34, introduced a wider range of subjects including about eighty from William Combe's books of the *Three Tours of Dr. Syntax* illustrated by Rowlandson and about twenty of Don Quixote. They even sought to capture the elaborate small detail of David Wilkie pictures including such popular subjects as "The Valentine" and "The Letter of Introduction" and printed in red, brown and black in their late years, with a keen eye for the dresser plate-rack that was perforce the cottager's picture gallery.

To a curious extent, however, the leading potters concentrated their attention on the American market, even including the American eagle and the famous E PLURIBUS UNUM in some of their marks. Andrew Stevenson from about 1812 and Ralph a few years later were early in this field as were Joseph Stubbs, the Ridgway firm and E. Wood before 1820 and William Adams of Stoke, S. Tams, J. & T. Edwards and J. Jackson through the 1830s. T. Godwin is noted for stone china toddy bowls, William Adams for his Columbus series, T. Mayer for his rare series showing the arms of some American states.

There is no end to this subject, ranging from bridge and pagoda fantasy to the entirely factual view of "New York from Weehawk", for example, taken from an on-the-spot drawing by the English artist W. G. Wall working for Andrew Stevenson and engraved by I. Hill. Probably sociologists can best explain the contrasting moods of a Wedgwood scene of romantic ruins, a violent series of big-game hunting by Spode adapted from *Oriental Field Sports* and, say, the forbidding New York Alms Houses by Ridgway. Assuredly there is nothing today comparable with their unselfconscious self-revelation. Yet the willow pattern continues unchallenged. Even the gorgeous Broseley dragon of J. & G. Rogers (1802–42) is almost forgotten— and indeed ceramic dragons could challenge the questing powers of the most adventurous collector. But the colour once known to its users as Broseley blue, zaffres blue, Canton blue or bamboo blue is instantly known and welcomed to this day by the term willow blue.

Chapter Eleven

MOCHA AND BANDED WARE

A HUNDRED years ago a dozen pint mugs for ale in mocha ware could be bought for tenpence. They were sturdy and easily made, colourful, clean, with strong clear glaze to protect their curiously spontaneous-looking ornament. It is certain that they were manufactured by innumerable potters in vast quantities for almost a century and, indeed, are still being produced on a small scale today. Yet now the collector swoops on even the humblest specimens. More surprising still, comparatively few people seem to have heard of the ware, still less to have handled any or speculated how potters applied the unique ornament, always with a fairly close similarity of pattern but never on two pieces identical.

Only the name is associated with the Arabian Red Sea port of Mocha and this merely because that was the port which shipped the finest quality of moss agates required by English Georgian jewellers. Fibrous material has created mossy patterns in tones of rust and green in this milky agate quartz, and an obvious although unintentional resemblance was noticed in what came to be known to potters as mocha ware, but to the public as tree or moss or seaweed work. One might even be tempted to think the name no more than a Victorian aggrandizement but that the authority on 19th century ceramics, Llewellyn Jewitt, noted an invoice of earthenwares made by Lakin, Poole & Shrigley which specified mocha tumblers by that name as early as 1792. The term occurs, too, in an 1836 list of Staffordshire workmen's prices. There is evidence, however, that some firms in their day-to-day records used merely the term "dipped ware" without specific reference to mocha.

For once it seems probable that the discovery of a process of decoration with practical commercial potential came by chance. The ornament depends upon the way a suitable mixture of acid liquid will creep and spread by capillary attraction in innumerable fine wavering lines through an appropriate wet dip or slip—a fine earthenware mixture of creamy consistency washed thinly over the surface of common ware before glazing. This application of an opaque slip or dip was a usual practice with cheap earthenwares: the dip was applied to the piece of ware after shaping, but before firing in the oven, filling in the uneven surface and providing a smooth, fine-grained basis for ornament.

A drop of the diffusing liquid was dabbed on to the dip while it was still thoroughly wet. On an inverted vessel the force of gravity produced what would appear as a tree pattern; on a vessel held horizontally, a feather pattern. With clever use of a blowpipe the potter could direct the flow more exactly to produce graceful curls and flower head effects in the same free, casual manner. But it is probably right to assume this was largely children's work. Charles Dickens, describing the W. T. Copeland factory in 1852, noted a man applying the band of wet slip and his daughter turning and tilting the vessel so that the blotches of blue she dropped from her brush ran into "rude images of trees", a comparatively leisurely, happy pastime for an imaginative but unskilled child of that desperately overworked period.

It is assumed that a careless workman, chewing tobacco, chanced upon the reactions of the acidic brown stain upon the wet alkaline dip. Subsequently infusions containing hops, tansy or lemon juice might form the basis of "mocha tea", richly stained brown with iron or manganese, blue with cobalt or more rarely green with chrome—the metallic oxides widely used for ceramic ornament. The date of the discovery is unknown, however, and dating of specimens is difficult since potters rarely marked such everyday wares. The earliest known piece with a date is a christening mug recorded by Haggar. This is inscribed M CLARK 1799: the inscription is beneath the glaze so it must have been painted on in the course of manufacture and not added later by a china seller. The ware is coarse and light, which tallies with its date, but the ornament is quite good: obviously production must have begun well before this date. The popularity of this ornament seems to have waned again late in the 19th century and by 1910 few mocha potters remained.

Obviously such casual decoration was mainly the work of potters in a small way of business and confined to inexpensive wares and it seems fairly certain that it was introduced to provide additional interest to the colourful but completely impersonal ornament of the general class of workaday crockery known as banded ware. Nevertheless, the important Teulon Porter collection, which supplied the illustrations to this brief survey and is now in the Stoke City Museum, includes two bowls of comparatively costly bone china and some earthenware pieces of considerable quality such as a graceful quart-size coffee pot and a tiny teapot (black "trees" on a yellow ground with flanking bands of blue) certainly intended for better than cottage or tavern use. Indeed, one of the interesting features of this ware is the wide assortment of pieces known to have been made in it and the hope, with considerable justification, that it may be possible still to find types hitherto unrecorded while collectors are few and the general public largely unacquainted with the ware's potentialities.

Ale pots, of course, were an obvious outlet, clean and bright alternatives to time-honoured, time-blackened pewter and only outmoded when clearer liquors were matched by tough vessels of glass. But a wide range of jugs was made, some of two- or three-gallon capacity. Some were made so large that the back handle had to be augmented by a finger grip at the front, but others are no more than 3-inch delights for dolls. There are toilet ewers and basins and a range of pots and bowls for kitchen goods, covered bowls for sugar, pots for butter and lard—favourites, it appears, with customers in the West Midlands. Here again the dolls' house equipment that occasionally comes to light suggests that eventually a still wider range of shape and purpose may be assembled. Sets for pepper, salt and mustard are parti-

23. Interesting variations by Spode of the familiar willow pattern and similarly transfer-printed underglaze in blue. The comport above dating to about 1790 shows only two figures on the bridge. The plate below dates to about 1808, known as the temple and landscape pattern. The butterfly border is extremely ornate.

24. Useful wares splendidly enriched with transfer printing in underglaze blue. *Top left:* Spode plate of about 1810 in the Tiber pattern showing one of three views of Rome. *Top right:* plate marked SPODE of about 1815 superbly printed in the Filigree pattern. *Centre:* the spill vase (*left*) shows Spode's Tower pattern; the jug has the mark of S. Barker, the Don Pottery. *Bottom left:* Spode comport of about 1820 in the British Flowers pattern: each piece in this service shows a different flower composition. *Bottom right:* jug in the pleasant shape of the 1820s, one of a set with different patterns from the Spode Botanical series.

cularly attractive, typically with blue trees on a white band flanked by yellow and favourites, it seems, in East Anglia. There are egg cups, too, and the rarer tea cup and its high-rimmed saucer, and there are spill vases for the mantleshelf.

Mainly, it must be noted, these pieces tend to be suitable for shaping on the potter's wheel, for the obvious reason that banded ornament was developed for such designs. In early specimens one notes bands of blue, yellow and dark brown, the range of colours being increased in the 19th century to include slate green, dark green, olive green, warm chestnut brown, red, orange, buff and grey. But towards the end of Victorian days the usual scheme was a mocha pattern in dark brown upon a band of grey flanked by bands of blue.

These bands of colour are often strikingly effective on specimens of mocha's heyday. They were applied in substantial creamy liquid dip similar to that which usually carried the mocha ornament. Their neat perfection implies a clever eye and a steady hand, as the colour was projected from a funnelled can on to the vessel revolving on the potter's wheel. For this work the potter or decorator used an old Chinese method, placing the dip in a globular vessel and forcing it out by means of two spouts or quills. By blowing down one spout into the vessel he projected the dip from the other at a controllable speed. In 1811 Richard Waters took out a patent for a time-saving method of applying three colours at once, using a three-section vessel with a three-section spout. This applied three parallel adjoining bands of different colours at once but required even more skilful sleight of hand when the decorator came to the end of each triple encircling band.

The bands of coloured clay dip were substantial and, of course, opaque and may feel slightly rounded to the finger tips. When they were dry, but before the whole vessel was covered with glaze, the potter could trim away any surplus blobs of colour by tooling on the wheel. For the most rudimentary banding, of course, it was possible to dip the whole vessel in a coloured slip, allow it to dry and then lathe-tool away surplus colour to leave a series of bands. These could then be augmented by the banding method described above, so as to provide a broad central band of wet dip for the mocha ornament. After having been submerged in clear liquid glaze the vessel was fired in the kiln, rendering body, ornament and glaze tough enough to endure the buffeting of ale house or cottage kitchen.

Banding was mentioned by William Evans in 1846 in his *Art and History of the Potting Business* where he described the "mocha fritted glaze". His formula consisted of Cornish stone twenty-six parts, litharge (monoxide of lead) fifty parts, flint (calcined) eleven parts and frit thirteen parts. This glassy frit was prepared from seventy parts of glass, twenty-two parts of litharge, four parts each of nitre and arsenic and one part of blue calx (cobalt oxide). Such ingredients had been used separately or in less elaborate combinations for many earlier glazes. The result was hard and strong but today often shows the fine cracks known as crazing. These indicate imperfect adjustment of glaze to body ingredients and hence their unequal reaction to atmospheric changes.

The familiar form of slip ware known as marbling was a concurrent method of decoration used on similar workaday vessels. Lines or splashes of opaque slips in different colours were dabbed on with a sponge and encouraged to intermingle on the vessel in streaks and waves. Such a surface while wet could be equally receptive for the mocha pattern, and such combined decoration is interesting and fairly rare, even though neither kind of ornament can really be said to enhance the other.

The early mocha which feels light in the hand was made in the cream-coloured earthenware that began to become important to English potters in the 1770s. As I have explained in Chapter Seven Josiah Wedgwood had challenged the monopoly of the Bristol porcelain maker, Richard Champion, and as a result the porcelain ingredients Cornish clay and china stone became available for potters working in earthenwares. This resulted in everyday wares of finer quality than had been possible hitherto and was a development of enormous value. But it is more usual to find mocha ornament on the harder, whiter pearl ware that became popular in the 1780s. The lightweight cream ware continued to be used to some extent until 1815 for export mocha, however, as Continental and North American excise duties were calculated by weight: collectors in the States, too, are beginning to discover these export pieces though not yet, I understand, by their English name.

Towards 1830 stonewares were used for some mocha pieces. An occasional specimen has been noted with bands of coloured slip at rim and base but with a band of thinner wash—ground-laid to the potter—containing the mocha pattern, and such a basis for the mocha is not rare in late work. The Teulon Porter collection includes large jugs in cane-coloured stoneware with mocha patterns in blue on encircling bands of white. These are thought to have come from the Kirkcaldy Pottery, Fifeshire, Scotland (at work through most of the 19th century), the mocha patterns having been shaped with a blowpipe to suggest conventionalized thistles. The Ridgway firm in the 1830s developed more heat-resistant stonewares so that quart mugs and the like could be used for the mulled beer that must have cracked innumerable pots when the red-hot poker was inexpertly applied. Some mugs are found with their handles insulated by bindings of cane or wicker.

It is interesting to note that mocha ware was among the products of the Creil factory, France. This pottery was established in about 1794 by an Englishmen, Bagnal; but nothing more is known of the man. His products were decidedly English, including transfer-printed earthenwares, some with English subjects, but homely mocha ware is a more surprising choice. The pottery was merged with Montereau early in the 19th century.

From the 1850s tough, heavy, workaday granite ware was used for many of the mugs and measures that were then the main preoccupation of the potters still producing mocha. Unfortunately such firms are mostly impossible to identify, since makers' marks are as rare on this as on such other attractive everyday wares as lustre. In the Teulon Porter collection one quart mug is marked with a pink rose, a mark that turns up from time to time in Devon and Cornwall but is impossible to associate with the potter John Rose of Coalport. Another mug is marked Edge, Malkin & Co.,

Burslem, a firm that was active between 1870 and 1903. Of the many other makers the only known firms are Pinder, Bourne & Co., Burslem (c.1860–80); Robert Maling and his successors, Newcastle-upon-Tyne (established 1817), who continued the manufacture of mocha ware until about 1914; and John Tams, Longton (1874–1912). Tams in 1889 advertised "The Excelsior Government Stamped Earthenware Measure" which he had patented and marked some of his mugs "Patent Government Stamp Measure Sole Patentee and Maker John Tams Longton Staffs".

Measures are intriguing for the collector. Mocha ware mugs designed for selling shellfish, birdseed and the like tended to give shamefully short-measure gills and half-pints, but in 1824 the imperial system of weights and measures was introduced and the tavern keepers' measures then had to show they had been officially tested. The potter indicated the capacity of his vessel, usually in the course of manufacture, before glazing, and the weights and measures officer added his verification stamp. Not until 1878 did the Board of Trade order that the marks used in different districts should be standardized and it was some years after that before all districts conformed.

In mocha ware the most interesting measures are those of the years 1824 to 1878. Some of these continue something of the age-old tradition whereby lords of the manor, guilds and similar people and bodies were responsible for authenticating weights and measures, using marks that often included details from their crests. Occasionally a vessel with an attractively ornate little plaque or seal may be found shaped in relief and attached to the measure before glazing. This may say no more than the word IMPERIAL, more or less decoratively, but it may indicate capacity also. Some potters gave their seals the crown and monarch's cypher of officialdom as well as indicating capacity, although this was against the law. As often, however, the seal is little better than a lopsided blob and in any case the practice was discontinued when the Board of Trade's standardized mark came to be accepted.

Instead of applying a seal, some potters indicated capacity on a measure by impressing the word upon the surface or

25a. Mocha ware showing the characteristic feather or tree patterns achieved by letting the colour creep through the bands of creamy dip. In its heyday the colours included blue, yellow, red, orange, grey, greens and browns.

25b. Jugs and mugs are among the most usual finds but the collector looks too for children's toy pieces, spill vases and vessels for condiments. The coffee pot is exceptionally attractive.

26a. Mocha ware on massive jugs showing the elaboration of flower fantasy that could be achieved by guiding the flow of colour with a blow pipe.

26b. Feather effects between bands of contrasting colours such as are familiar on the cottager's banded ware. In the mug *lower left* the background is a marbled slip that tends to obscure the mocha pattern.

the unfired earthenware or by painting it, in both cases
protecting it from wear by covering it with glaze, just as
some public-house keepers had their names or the names of
their houses inscribed underglaze on jugs and mugs. A less
usual mark that occasionally turns up has a faint line inside
the brim and on the outside the declaration that the vessel
holds a "PINT UP TO THE COLOURED LINE INSIDE". Edge,
Malkin & Co. made some that were marked in this way. The
Board of Trade also accepted a nick or slot in the rim above
the handle to reduce capacity to the exact measure required,
but stipulated that this must not go more than three-eighths
of an inch below the rim.

The other mark to look for on the early pint or quart pot
is the officer's verification of the capacity claimed by the
potter, all too long accustomed to meet his customers'
orders for short measures. It is interesting to note the
various ways the officers introduced, experimentally, for
attaching marks that would stand up to years of rough
usage. One early official mark is a band of zinc stamped with
the capacity—such as QT IMP—and wrapped round the
handle of the vessel: this is fixed with solder on the inner
side and given authority by being stamped here with the
monarch's cypher and a district number or other distin-
guishing motif—N 7 for Nottingham has been noted. The
Stoke motif before 1878 was a swan above a Staffordshire
knot.

Alternatively a verification stamp might be inserted at the
base of the handle or riveted under the lip. This is found as a
little round plug of metal, often worn almost smooth if of
lead, but more enduringly marked when of copper. Or there
may be a mark in the centre of the vessel's base. The official
mark approved by the Board of Trade in 1878 and eventually accepted everywhere consisted of a royal crown over
the monarch's cypher and the number of the county or
borough. Such a mark is often found on a vessel dating
many years earlier, so that the cypher VR, ER or GR indicates
testing rather than manufacture during the reign of that
monarch. The number indicates the county or borough of
the testing officer concerned—522 for London County, for
example, nineteen for Derby County, ten for Cornwall,

sixty-four for Sunderland, 254 for Berkshire and thirty-two for the important Staffordshire Potteries area. A letter below may be a clue to the officer concerned or, as in the important pot-making centre of Newcastle (seventy-one), the date of testing. Eventually, too, the Board of Trade found a satisfactory method of applying their mark, using a stencil and removing the glaze either with acid or by sandblasting. Wear tended to make the mark more conspicuous, as without glaze the earthenware body was susceptible to every sort of stain. Nowadays capacity, too, is included in this official mark.

Curiously enough, although such an important North Country firm as Maling of Newcastle included mocha mugs among its products, this tree ware appears to have been almost wholly a Midlands and south of England fancy.

Chapter Twelve

———————

WHEN today's children find their breakfast entertainment on their packets of cereals who are we to scoff at
the Victorian delight in applying unrelated ornament to
articles that by modern rules would not be ornamented at
all? We think in terms of short-lived card, however, while
Victorians had the self-assurance to make their trivia last.

Today any antiques collector who concentrates on the
more homely pieces, adaptable if not actually born to
cottage life, soon realizes that decorative detail is mainly
to be found in ceramic wares. Oven-fired colours under
strong clear glazes defied all the extremes of atmospheric
disruption. Pictures may crack, furniture warp, but with no
more than a slight mellowing these plates and plaques and
personally inscribed loving cups submit unconditionally to
the new hazards that we live among today. The cottager of
yesterday who propped a picture pot-lid upon the mantelshelf for the sake of its glint of colour or pretty theme might
be surprised to find how many collectors today respond
gladly to the same absurd notions—still more astonished to
see modern fake lids often in poorer tones and artificially
crazed cherished by the undiscriminating.

Modern opinion might shy at the thought of a royal
occasion commemorated on a jar of hair lotion or a Picasso
reproduced on a pot of shrimp paste. But we accept
Victorian pot-lids decorated with copies of favourite
contemporaneous pictures even though everyone nowadays
knows that they originated merely as the covers of pots
containing fish and meat pastes and hair pomades. Look
in any window of curios—just too late to rank yet as
antiques—and almost certainly the display will include one

or two of these pictorial trifles. Some are complete with their shallow pots although they do not always appear to have begun life together.

These slightly rounded lids of white glazed earthenware, 3 to 6 inches in diameter, have as their sole claim to distinction their multi-coloured decoration. But this is indeed noteworthy. The man who first decorated these pot-lids achieved no less than a new commercial decorative process, even if his own personal success amounted to no more than a yearly salary of £175. Today a single rare, early specimen of his work may cost over a hundred pounds and the least ambitious example probably two pounds or more. Inevitably there are many reproductions about, too, but usually these can be distinguished fairly easily.

The early Victorian dandy deluged his hair with bear's grease pomade and macassar oil preparations, bought in shallow earthenware pots which were printed in black, under the glaze, with details of their contents. When, in the mid-1830s, similar little pots were used for packing fish pastes, the flat lids were covered with glued-on paper labels, which did show some attempt at decorative effect, with printed engravings. But the first direct step towards the full-colour picture pot-lid was the idea of applying a printed transfer-engraving directly to the pottery lid. As I have shown in Chapter Ten this monochrome transfer process had long been used by the pottery trade for pictorial work and as a basis for hand colouring. The process that originated on these quaint little lids consisted in building up each fully coloured picture entirely by the use of a multi-coloured transfer print.

The firm making the pots for the hair dressing known as bear's grease was F. & R. Pratt of Fenton, Staffordshire, and it was this firm's chief decorator, Jesse Austin (1806–79), who in 1845 lit upon the idea of decorating them by making vari-coloured pictures with transfers. When he died no one was ever found to replace him.

Austin was an expert engraver of the copper plates required for printing the transfer papers used for ceramic work. He had served his apprenticeship with the notably progressive potter John Davenport of Longport and at the age of twenty-one had established himself as a designer and copper-plate engraver to the trade. By the late 1830s this freelance work was no longer in any great demand and Austin closed his workshops in 1840, on finding work with the Pratt firm.

Colour printing was in everyone's mind in these early Victorian days. In Chapter Nineteen I mention the success of George Baxter's printing of superimposed colours which probably influenced Austin's ideas. But Austin himself possessed the artist's ability to separate a picture into its component primary colours which I discuss in that chapter. A separate copper plate was engraved for each major colour and tint: blue, red, pink and buff were frequently used, never more than four for a single picture in addition to outlines in brown and all able to be fixed by a single firing in the kiln. What has not been realized by most collectors, and was first recorded by G. Bernard Hughes in 1959, is that the building up of the colours, by printing from the different copper plates in perfect register one over the other, was achieved on the transfer paper. Thus one paper conveyed all the colours together to the ware.

The use of such a revolutionary multi-colour transfer was indicated by comment at the 1851 Exhibition and confirmed by various patent specifications referring to "the order in which the colours are ordinarily printed upon the transfer paper". The brown outlines that completed and sharpened the picture were introduced in a full line and stipple engraving, only the flesh parts being stippled: this was printed first upon the transfer paper and so appears over the colours on the pot-lid. For the best results the colours were allowed to become nearly dry upon the paper before the paper was applied to the biscuit earthenware coated with a suitably receptive varnish. The pottery used was a close-textured, vitreous earthenware, non-absorbent, so that the colours printed upon it show in full brilliance upon the surface, protected by the subsequent glazing. From a commercial point of view it was quicker to prepare and apply these colours by transfer to large quantities of lids than to apply colour by hand with comparable delicacy.

As in any transfer work, the tissue paper was washed off

when its load of colours had been transferred to the lid and time allowed for drying. The really important technical detail was the perfect placing of the colours to avoid any blurring. This was aided by using register marks to the sides of each engraving. As the plates were applied to the paper these marks were exactly superimposed. Three or four register marks around a single lid may be noted occasionally. Such marks—tiny rings—are often faintly discernible beneath the border of ornament or gilding that usually surrounds any but the earliest style of lid. They are not to be confused with the slightly raised patches sometimes found on a picture which result from touching up by hand. It may be mentioned that the copper plates used for such a multi-colour transfer often became the customer's property. The Banger accounts show that they might cost more than twenty pounds the set, presumably including Austin's original painting—and he was a considerable artist in water colour.

When the colour work was complete the lids were placed in hardening kilns at a temperature great enough to burn all oil from the coloured printing inks. They were then ready for the final process of glazing that gave the little pictures their permanence.

At first only two colours were used and since the hair dressing known as bear's grease was contained in the pots Austin's first thought was to produce pictures featuring bears: by early in 1846 "Polar Bears" in two colours was on the market. The now rare and comparatively simple bear series ran to sixteen subjects, such as "Bears at School", "Performing Bears" and the like, Austin progressively improving his printing methods until the later examples were in four colours. Some, dating from about 1850 onwards, are found with the pomade maker's name and address surrounding the picture. For instance, there is a bear-hunting scene accompanied by the words "Ross & Sons' Genuine Bear's Grease Perfumed. 119 & 120 Bishopsgate Street, London".

The earliest style of pot-lid was flat and its uneven, dappled surface was ill-suited to transfer printing, but is now all the rarer and more highly valued. In December 1847 Felix Pratt was granted a patent for his method of mechanically shaping a lid with a perfectly smooth, slightly convex surface. It was on lids of this kind that picture transfer-printing was developed.

What do collectors look for among a miscellaneous assortment of pot-lids? In addition to the early bear subjects, signed lids are desirable. Some fifty pictures were designed by Austin and signed *J. Austin Sc.* or *J.A.Sc.* The name *T. Jackson*, a now forgotten artist, has been noted on four lid designs. Sometimes a maker's mark is found. But the mark that more often puzzles the collector is the diamond-shaped registration mark used occasionally as protection against copyists between 1842 and 1883. The figures and letters indicate the date that the pattern was registered and make it possible to find the name of the originators. Such registration gave three years' protection against copying. This mark may be worked into the design of the picture or impressed inside the lid, while on the base of the pot there is usually a black underglaze announcement of its original contents.

The earliest pot-lids to be decorated for the fish-paste trade were commissioned by Tatnell & Son and S. Banger, both of Pegwell Bay near Ramsgate. Naturally they wanted decorations associated with their famous shrimp pastes, the result being an attractive series of lids bearing pictures of the Pegwell Bay district.

Pot-lid pictures were usually issued in series, their subjects fascinatingly typical of their period. Here are to be found not only the obvious bear motifs and nautical scenes but pictures of celebrities, views of the Great Exhibition, of London and other picturesque places, military scenes, sports and pastimes. Inevitably there was a series for Shakespeare enthusiasts and many were the copies of popular paintings. There are about twenty views in the London series, Buckingham Palace and Westminster Abbey now being rarities. The words "Entered at Stationers' Hall" are printed on four of the series: the Tower, St. Paul's Cathedral, Westminster Abbey and the Houses of Parliament. No other designs possess this copyright-protecting inscription and such pieces are valued accordingly.

Sports and pastimes contributed some extremely attractive

lids including "Hide and Seek", "Snapdragon" and "A Pair" showing an old man and woman playing cribbage. But there were no limits to Austin's ambitious efforts. His copying of paintings by well-known artists even included Gainsborough's "Blue Boy". Other familiar works by Royal Academicians reproduced in this way are Mulready's "The Last In", Wilkie's "Blind Fiddler", Landseer's "Highland Music", T. Webster's "Truant" and W. Witherington's "Hop Queen".

Surprisingly, perhaps, many a pot-lid collector appears to be unaware of the wide range of Staffordshire pottery that was decorated with full-colour pictures in the same way. This includes wall plaques with gilded rims, toilet-table pots, trinket sets, jugs, mugs, vases, plates and dishes. Here again well-known paintings were blithely reproduced, but the majority were exported to America where they had a considerable vogue. Success prompted the Pratt firm to issue tea-sets. Every teapot and every tea cup had two different pictures on its sides, rimmed with burnished gold. Sometimes a plate is found with a pot-lid picture as its central decoration framed in the familiar printed border patterning of Staffordshire blue.

At the Great Exhibition this "new process in ceramics decoration" was highly regarded. In addition to the Pratts, the firm of T. J. & J. Mayer produced such pictures, mostly on domestic ware, but including more than fifty pot-lid designs, and of course every design appeared on many lids. Another firm that issued pot-lids at some time during the 1850s had the unwieldy name of T. C. Brown-Westhead, Moore & Company of Shelton. Their products bear witness to the fact that Jesse Austin had a disagreement with the Pratt firm and for about a year was employed by this rival. It is satisfactory to record that Austin won the day. He had been his own chemist and colour-maker and the Pratts found it impossible to duplicate his formula and methods. The new competition and the decline in the quality of "Pratt's coloured pictures on pottery" prompted the firm to persuade Austin to return at a salary of £175 a year.

Shortly afterwards his employers succeeded in gaining

27. Picture pot-lids decorated by Jesse Austin for the firm of F. & R. Pratt of Fenton. *Upper left:* "Bears at School" from the early series of sixteen bear subjects intended for the lids of pots containing bear's grease hair pomade. This is found in several versions and in a re-issue. *Upper right:* "Sandringham, the Seat of H.R.H. the Prince of Wales". The view dates between 1862 and 1872, and was drawn and engraved by Austin. *Lower left:* a naïve view of Samuel Banger's shrimp paste and sauce factory at Pegwell Bay, Ramsgate. As the pots so lidded would contain his shrimp paste the shop windows and the notice boards above concentrate on announcing the sauce, while a shrimper with net and thigh boots approaches the door. *Lower right:* a late example, "Osborne House, Isle of Wight" which became a royal residence in 1875, three years before Austin's death.

28. Austin work on pot-lids, vase and dessert plates. *Top:* "I see you, my boy", signed J. A.; "The Game Bag." *Centre:* rare lid showing the Prince of Wales at Washington's tomb, 1860; "The Trooper" from a pair of vases shown at the 1851 Exhibition. *Bottom:* reproductions of famous paintings—W. F. Witherington's "Hop Queen" and T. Webster's "Truant".

the interest of the firm of Crosse & Blackwell. Results were so good that the competing firms of E. Lazenby & Son and John Burgess quickly followed. These three firms issued many thousands of pots with these colourful lids each year, covering more than 400 different subjects, until Jesse Austin's death in 1879, when a successor to replace him was sought in vain.

Some 200 of the 500 original sets of copper plates used by the Pratt firm were rediscovered early in the present century. When pot-lids began to be collected re-issues from some of the original sets of plates were made, but in a harder earthenware. The collector must be on guard, therefore, to distinguish re-issues from originals. Early lids display rich velvety colour effects and the reds and blues have a brilliance and body depth lacking in the more modern productions. Detail work was more meticulous too. The surface of a Victorian lid made before the 1880s is usually crazed, the term for a covering or network of irregular hair-lines resembling fine cracks—finer than the artificial crazing found on some modern specimens. Among some thirty portraits recorded on pot-lids at least ten were re-issued early this century and these have now had time to weather and may be taken as originals. These are: "The Late Prince Consort", "The Prince and Princess of Wales", "The Duke of Wellington", "The Allied Generals", "Garibaldi", "The Meeting of Garibaldi and Victor Emmanuel", "England's Pride", "The Blue Boy", "Sir Robert Peel" and "Peabody".

Pot-lids can be tested by their tone. The collector hangs a questionable lid from the little finger and taps it with another lid. Provided it is not cracked a dull sound should indicate a 19th century specimen. Uncracked lids of more recent manufacture may emit a clear, bell-like note, although if artificially crazed or otherwise "antiqued" the ring is less distinct. However, even to this rule there is an occasional exception, for a few Victorian lids by the Ridgway firm of the Cauldon Pottery were made in bone china and so have a clear ring.

How Jesse Austin would chuckle today to see his humble products tested in this way.

Chapter Thirteen

EARLY BRASS AND COPPER

THOSE of us who rejoice in the gleam of brass and copper are liable perhaps to credit too bright a sparkle to the everyday fittings of the early English home. It has to be admitted that in all the essentials of lighting, heating, cooking, washing, the metal that did most of the work was iron. Collectors must pick warily among brass and copper items lacking any authentic purpose in the Tudor, Stuart or Georgian household, most especially among clumsy brass pieces shaped by casting. Here as in all branches of collecting there is no substitute for seeing and handling authentic pieces of known date and pedigree, noting subtleties of colour, of surface texture, of finish on exposed and hidden parts, noting signs of wear that correspond with the article's purpose rather than to ease of its application to a polishing wheel.

In crafts producing everyday wares generation after generation it was inevitable that traditional designs and manufacturing methods should linger. One may perhaps accept that much late Victorian work on traditional lines tends to be credited to an earlier century but nothing can mitigate the disappointment of being caught by a shoddy modern reproduction made for ornament rather than use. Cast brass chestnut roasters may be mentioned, for example, mimicking the perforated iron box on a long handle and with a second long handle to the hinged lid that could be thrust into the embers. Still worse is an oddity thought up by a manufacturer who hopes that purchasers will find their own explanations to justify its existence.

For any useful survey it is important first to be clear about the terms used in old records that indicate the scope of the subject. And it must be admitted at once that little domestic work of any quality was made of native brass or copper until at least the very end of the 17th century. For some notion of the wares then available it is necessary of course to search the records of prosperous households rather than the cottager's primitive equipment. In 1590, for example, Sir Thomas Ramsey, former Lord Mayor of London, owned fifty-eight brass candlesticks and kitchen-wares of latten, brass, pewter and iron but his only piece of copper was a "kettle" weighing thirty pounds. The will of Henry Bright in 1638 recorded brass utensils including two pots, eight kettles, three skillets, a frying pan, a skimmer, three candlesticks, a pestle and mortar and a baking pan. But the English copper industry was neglected and English brass made from it was a "scurvy" alloy according to the men who tried to shape it into finished goods. For anything as important as a warming pan lid they chose Dutch or Flemish latten.

Then in the 1690s copper mining was revived and this was followed in the 1720s by conspicuous advances in its purification. As early as 1708 the Company of Armourers and Braziers acquired the right to search out faulty work in and around London and before the mid-18th century English braziers and coppersmiths had overcome any need for Continental imports of domestic wares. Improvements in copper smelting to remove damaging impurities such as sulphur were important to coppersmiths hammering out fine copper vessels but far more important to the makers of its alloys—brass, bronze, pinchbeck and prince's metal, bath metal, German or nickel silver, Dutch metal, speculum.

The costly alloy bronze consisted basically of copper alloyed with tin. It was easier to cast than copper but an occasional 17th century cooking pot, a massive mortar or decorative andiron gave it scant place in the everyday home. Furniture mounts cast in bronze and gilded —ormolu—were a rich luxury easily forgone in favour of brass. Speculum, made with copper, tin and traces of other minerals, was long used for the so-called steel mirrors in patch boxes and the like. Prince Rupert's metal—prince's metal—invented in the 1670s and Christopher Pinchbeck's renowned substitute for gold were costly forms of burnished brass with much the tone of gold. Dutch metal was a brass substitute for gold leaf. Britannia metal and nickel silver were alloys that eventually rivalled pewter and ousted pure copper in the manufacture of plated silver (see Chapter Seventeen).

For the home, however, the important early alloy was brass, composed at that time of copper and the ore of zinc known as calamine. From 1770 brass could be made by combining copper with metallic zinc—spelter—instead of zinc ore. This is today's method but it was more like 1860 before this improvement became general.

In early documents the brass wares are often detailed merely as "yellow" but something more exact is implied by the use of the term latten. This specified brass plate of a strong, close-textured quality flattened from the ingot by batteries of water-driven hammers, a process brought to England from Germany in the 1580s. Flemish latten was long favoured since even when shaped by casting the early English brass showed pitting that could not be removed entirely by the finishing process of turning on the lathe and flaws that could result in fractures. In the 1690s, however, it was made more pliable as well as somewhat lighter in colour by adding a little lead. Thimble casting became an important minor trade, producing the various shapes of thumb and finger guard needed by the many different craftsmen who hand sewed fabrics and leather.

Improvements in casting methods came in the 18th century but the really conspicuous advances were in the rolling mills where in 1728 John Cook patented a rolling machine fitted with compression springs. The resultant brass and copper sheets were a far more amenable material for the brazier and coppersmith than earlier English products and many a street of open-fronted workshops echoed to the busy clangour as they planished their metal sheet to improve texture by endless sonorous hammering and fashioned their vessels by the early method of "raising" them into rounded shapes "as women make pies" as John Houghton had described it in 1697.

Heavy battery hammering was continued for thick sheets

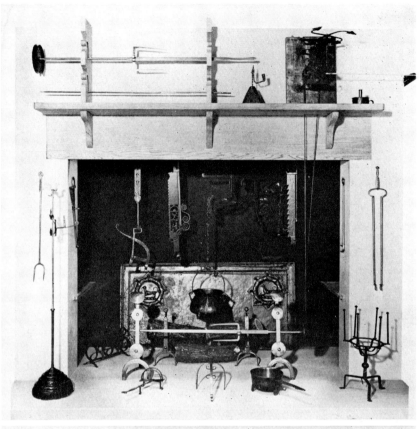

29. An English down-hearth. Details shown include spit dogs supporting a meat spit and flanking the brand dogs holding the firewood. From left to right above the rectangular fireback are a kettle tilter, decorated pot-hook, elaborate chimney crane which can suspend the "kettle" or cooking pot over any part of the fire, and simpler pot-hook. On the shelf above are a spit in its rack and the clockwork spit jack to keep the spit turning in front of the fire. In the foreground from extreme left are a floor rushlight holder, bread toasters, posnet and wrought iron stand for warming plates. *Below:* early 17th-century cast bronze posnet, its handle cast with the words YE WAGES OF SIN IS DEATH.

30. Small brassware of the 18th century with the elegance of silver plate. The covered box with essential perforated lid is 3½ inches high and intended for soap: every wash-basin stand of the period—now mistakenly listed as a wig-stand—had its soap-box recess. The snuffers and stand is a rare piece, the stand resembling a broad-footed candlestick in the hexagonal shaping of early Georgian silver but with a small lifting handle and shaped in the socket to hold the snuffer blades and the lidded box attached to them which received and quenched the snuff clipped from burning candles. The casters below, 9 inches high, are in the waisted octagonal shape with finely pierced lids of early Georgian days and the delightful cream jug has the jaunty outline associated with the 1750s.

of brass until steam power was applied to the rolling machines in the 19th century. But for the householder's everyday wares the development was highly important since it enabled the brass man to produce good working vessels and kitchen tools at prices ensuring a wide sale and so prompting a welcome extension of size and design to intrigue the collector.

For copper the improvement in the rolling mills coincided with increased efficiency in its smelting and refining by methods patented in 1725 and 1728 so that from the 1730s onwards it began to take its place with latten and brass in the English household—in those magnificent hot-water jugs for example that are often given far earlier dates. Soon English copper goods of glowing colour and soft smooth surface dominated the world markets. It may be mentioned here that progressive improvements in purifying the metal during the 18th century made rolled copper sheet a splendid material by the 1770s when copper ingots were in demand for the vastly important and wholly English trade of Sheffield plate and copper sheet was the essential basis for delectable little toys in English painted enamels. By 1850 it was freed from virtually all impurities but no longer in any great demand.

In brass the 18th century's major development was Emerson's success in making it by alloying the copper with the metallic zinc known as spelter. This splendid golden-toned brass was especially in demand for ornamental pieces cast and double gilded such as pastille burners and girandoles. These were clear and unpitted, comparable with work in pinchbeck or prince's metal. Nevertheless with the improved method of casting that evolved in the third quarter of the 18th century the older calamine brass remained in wide use for many everyday wares until the 1860s.

It is easy perhaps to give too great an emphasis to the triumph of Emerson's fine brass which only very gradually received the recognition it deserved. Most important eventually was its contribution to the high standard of quality that accompanied the later 18th century's development of revolutionary new production methods for brass and copper small wares. Richard Ford of Birmingham in 1769 patented the machine stamping process for shaping the metal sheet between hammers in corresponding concave and convex outline, a method first used for producing raised ornaments on small brass furniture fittings. Hollow blanks stamped by drop hammer in the factory could then be bought by small manufacturers for making up as required. Such blanks used less than a third the weight of metal required when shaping by hand hammering.

Reductions in the costs of both material and labour-time meant that the small manufacturer could lower his prices as well as widening his range of stock. For example, a hand-raised copper warming pan sold for about 11s. in 1770 but for less than 4s. in drop-stamped copper of the 1780s.

Yet another manufacturing technique was developed in the late 18th century to help the brazier and coppersmith seeking to produce cheap goods. This consisted of pressing the metal into the required hollow shape with a wooden form which was revolved on a lathe. Spun hollow ware is easily recognized by the encircling marks on the inside. A specially fine soft copper was developed for the process.

Many collectors prefer to avoid stamped and spun wares in both copper and brass but this is to deny the basic purpose of these wares as refreshingly light-reflecting, eye-pleasing household equipment that could stand up to everyday use in kitchen and cottage where silver had no place. Doubtless also they met the housewife's demands for a material that paraded its cleanliness or betrayed its neglect at a glance, but in fact the effects of acid foods upon copper and copper-alloys always worried medical men and real cleanliness inside the cooking pot depended upon careful and frequent tinning.

Randle Holme in the 17th century describes a saucepan of brass or copper "tinned all within which is to keep sauces or butter melted in it from brass-severing". Trenchers, the most primitive form of flat plate supplied to diners for cutting their meat at table, might be made of hard, battery-hammered copper when this became available. When tinned attractively they suggested silver but were far more resistant to knife marks. The early difficulty was to secure effective

tinning. John Bootie introduced an improved method in
1770 but even then results were far from satisfactory and in
1790 a patent was secured to "prevent corrosion of tinning
and all those noxious effects from brass and copper when
used for culinary purposes". Even the tin itself might be
suspect and in 1756 the Society of Arts stressed the danger
of tin which had been cheapened by adding lead and which
was no defence against food acids at a period when all
manner of potent pickles and spices were heaped upon
winter's dried and salted foods.

English brass and copper ware throughout the collector's
period tends to be plain for easy cleaning and long service
but in immensely satisfying shapes because these were
craftsmen's interpretations of homely needs adjusted to
harmonize with current notions of fashion. Knowledge of
contemporaneous silver styles is often useful and enlighten-
ing, both to explain, say, the change from octagonal base to
a scalloped outline in an early Georgian candlestick and to
avoid ornate Continental work. To glimpse the range of
design that accompanied changes of process one has only to
survey the furniture fittings produced by the brassman from
the later 17th century onwards when something more
elegant than iron was required for the newly fashionable
surfaces of marquetry and veneer. Drawer handle and key
escutcheon trace the progress of the brassman from early
solid castings to hand-hammered surfaces ornamented to
mask their imperfections and thence to the lighter rolled
plate. This could be elaborately outlined and perforated and
was followed by the introduction of relief ornament shaped
by machine stamping. All this was accompanied of course by
changes of style from the earliest acorns and knobs through
the arching Queen Anne outlines, angular early Georgian
work, rococo chinoiserie and Gothic motifs of the mid-
18th century and subsequent neo-classic motifs. The years
around the Regency (1810–20) are associated with furniture
brasswork at its best as inlay, wire grills and ornamental
galleries and much of this attractive work was continued
far into Victorian days.

Today the collector has to accept the rarity of really early
copper and brass wares. Traditions of design and technique

can be traced even in 19th century work, however, and a brief summary of early brass and copper bygones may help the cottage dweller of today to understand how earlier generations sought pleasant, serviceable tools when preparing meals and providing the warmth and light that these homely metals respond to so richly.

In Tudor and Stuart England the log fire was served mainly by firedogs and creepers made of iron. Even in a rich household such as the Earl of Northampton's in 1614, the inventory lists andirons topped with copper and creepers topped with brass. The brass andirons or endirons that flanked the fire's essential supports were described with some justification by Fuller in 1662 as standing only for state. But they were decorative enough, often shaped as figures or demifigures such as cupids holding up shields of arms. By the mid-17th century personal emblems or shields were considered sufficient ornament and the early scrolling feet disappeared in favour of plain semicircular bases. In the later years of the century andirons became as ornate as other fittings, cast in brass or bronze. Even cast iron specimens might be faced and finished with perforated brass or copper—"fire grate, fire shovel, tongs and andirons all adorned with brass bobs and buttons" as observed in the well-appointed mid-Stuart dining room by the invaluable Randle Holme.

Dutch influence was manifest in fireside fittings of the century's end which included tapering brass andirons topped by urn or flame or acorn finials. Gadrooned ornament responded delightfully to the flicker of firelight and the turn of the century saw a liking for standards in many curved vase or baluster outlines, shaped by casting and finished on the lathe. Reductions in the fireplace size soon limited the demand for these ornaments but some may be noted in use as late as the 18th century flanking the barred grates often fitted into old down-hearth fireplaces and occasionally supporting the fire-irons.

More generally, brass and latten in the early down-hearth was restricted to what in the 1620s became known as a curfew. This massive half dome some 2 feet across, of iron or latten, could cover the simple down-hearth fire and be pushed neatly against the iron fireback. This met a regulation intended to prevent fire danger at night but its main advantage was that the fire could smoulder through the night and thus save the weary business of lighting it again in the morning. At its most elaborate the curfew might bear vigorous ornament in repoussé work.

Latten workers specializing in curfews made also the substantial ember pans of the early warming pans, supplying these to small brassmen who fitted them with the characteristic iron handles and decorative lids made from thin, high-quality Dutch or Flemish latten. Both the curfew and the early warming pan were substantial pieces that might be made in copper, as also were some big dish covers. It is interesting to note a reference to a curfew in the *Gentleman's Magazine* in 1779: "He has gotten a piece of household furniture of copper, which he was pleased to call a curfew . . . from its use of suddenly putting out a fire."

Dutch latten, comparatively flawless, in thin plates, may be noted in some other early household details such as the essential tinder box that contained the elaborate equipment for making a fire. Only in the kitchen was there much demand for early brass utensils and these are now little more than inventory records testifying to the considerable array of vessels and tools available to the cook to compensate for the shortcomings of the down-hearth or open fire. Most important additions to the fire were the wrought iron crane that could be swung across it for hanging pots on pot-hooks. Some were elaborate, allowing the cook to use all parts of the fire. The turn spit was improved too but undoubtedly the most decorative minor addition was the trivet.

In iron this "three square trivet or brandreth" was in general use from the 15th century, shaped as a hollow ring or triangle on three legs to hold the cauldron over or in front of the fire. When used in front of the fire for flat-bottomed latten saucepans it acquired a platform base perforated or cast in the same bright metal. The gridiron was another important utensil, usually of iron but sometimes of brass or silver to please the fastidious and then considered too precious for the heat of the down-hearth and used instead over a brazier of the fine charcoal known as court charcoal. A silver specimen made in Paris is mentioned in the *Paston Letters*, 1482.

Among cooking pots the most important were the substantial ''kettles'' or cauldrons made to hook on the range or crane across the fireplace. Some of the earliest were cast in bronze but by the 14th century many more were of iron. In Stuart days they were still mainly of iron but not exclusively: a large household would usually list a few among the kitchen brass ware. The brass cauldron was raised by hammering from the latten plate, usually in two parts with the brazed joint hidden by a strengthening rib. It was seldom fitted with legs as the cook had to adjust its height above the flames and this was done more conveniently by hanging it by its bail handle. Its contents of meat and vegetables were saved from burning by being placed in nets hung by hooks from the rim. For lack of an oven it could be placed among the embers for baking bread, which doubtless suggested the development of the Dutch or portable oven pushed into the fire on a long-handled iron brandreth.

Various soup pots were made. A typical style, listed in a catalogue of the early 1770s, was straight-sided with a close cover fitting tightly over it and dished to hold pewter soup plates to warm. This was made in fourteen sizes from 1 gallon to 17 and to specified weights. Saucepans for more individual cooking over a brazier or among the embers included footed posnets in various sizes, and pottage pans for the many spoon-supped stews of preserved meats. The term skillet is usually taken to imply a flat-based, footed saucepan, but it has been noted in Suffolk as a term for a milk skimmer and is given by Brogden as an ale-warmer.

The three-footed posnet dating from at least as early as the 13th century was particularly useful for making sauces and the like over a small brazier which itself might be of brass. At Barnard Castle in 1680 three brass posnets were valued at one shilling. In brass or copper the posnet was tinned inside but the epicure was served his buttered eggs and similarly lightly flavoured concoctions from posnets of silver. Early vessels may have curving handles but by the

18th century the handle was usually straight and tapering. Saucepans as such were listed by the latten tradesmen in 1620. They were hammered in latten through much of the 18th century and later produced by stamping in rolled brass. Henry Hamilton in *The English Brass and Copper Industries* noted specialist makers of frying pans by 1770. Other specialists included makers of brass nutcrackers and here again traditional styles have lingered. Some specimens much like those of today have been traced back to the 18th century, hinged together at the tips to get a direct squeezing action on the nippers instead of a scissors movement and with handles rounded out for a strong grip.

Another group of early fireside brass covers cooking tools—all the ladles and skimmers and plain and perforated slices required for open fire and brazier cookery. A typical skimmer consisted of a perforated disc of latten hammered into a shallow depression and mounted on a long iron handle looped for hanging on the wall. Short-handled skimmers for cream and the like were known as fleets or flits. Randle Holme in the 17th century described the plate of brass or copper or silver as 10 to 12 inches across "set orderly with holes that a rush may go through".

Spoons might be cast from brass or beaten from latten plate and when well tinned and burnished could be taken briefly for silver. Finials might be cast, brazed to the stems and gilded but among 17th century work the most usual styles were the successors to these endearing little pieces—the functional square or slant-cut slipped-in-the-stalk design and the subsequent flattened ends variously notched into small rounded projections and known as trifids. Towards the end of the 17th century the spoon end might have a large central arc curving upward at the tip flanked by two smaller arcs. This was enough of a favourite to acquire a name—the cat's head.

Chapter Fourteen

GEORGIAN BRASS AND COPPER

────────

THE early tentative use of brass and copper in the everyday English home and the way these splendid metals eventually took possession are described in the preceding chapter. By the 18th century brass was being welcomed in increasingly handsome table furnishings but the coppersmith only gradually contributed the warmer radiance now most especially admired. Admired as furnishings rather than for use, I must admit, and perhaps this is just as well for those who have never had to worry over the need for frequent re-tinning. Present-day non-stick surfaces have made us treat our saucepans with some respect once more, however, and restored the status of the wooden spoon.

Conspicuous metal ware on the dining table might include a wine cistern containing iced water for bottles of wine. Some in the 17th century were of Flemish latten. Others even then were of copper and the Howard accounts, for example referred in 1629 to a little copper cistern to set flagons in. This weighed 30½ lb. and cost £2 3s. 4d. In 1667 Samuel Pepys noted "the price of a copper cistern for the table, which is very pretty, and they demand £6 or £7 for one". This would be an isolated extravagance, but through Georgian days a well-equipped kitchen glowed bright with brass and copper. Every kind of cauldron, kettle, saucepan and dish cover appeared in abundance, long-proved production methods vying with new notions as the 18th century manufacturers revolutionized their trades. Thus, throughout the century and even as late as 1860 cauldrons were available and catalogued both in cast brass and in rolled plate.

Stamped brass ware became plentiful in the last twenty years of the century and spinning was developed for hollow-ware. Both copper and brass were used for tea kettle, coffee pot and chocolate pot and their stands, depending for their attraction on good design with a minimum of surface ornament. Brass plate coffee and chocolate pots may be found in capacities from 1 to 3 pints and spouted tea kettles were made from 3 pints to a gallon. A find indeed is an 18th century brass or copper tea kettle with its original heater and stand: instead of surface decoration the collector looks for well-proportioned detail such as shapely scrolling feet and a handle made of green stained ivory or covered in plaited cane.

Other attractive table pieces included cream jugs, as graceful as any in silver, and shapely sugar castors patterned in delicate perforations.

In copper vessels the list available for the mid-Georgian home would include some ten sizes of saucepan with upslanting handles of hard wood—often lignum vitae—pottage pots up to 14 gallons, soup pots, stew pans, pudding pans, frying pans and fish kettles with hoop handles and swivel eyes for hanging over the fire, jelly moulds, ale warmers. Of these the ale warmer is not always recognised, although many of the boot variety are of recent make. This vessel was used for preparing hot drinks, sweetened or spiced and sometimes enriched with egg yolk. The early boot design for a down-hearth had a cylindrical body, sometimes lidded, with a projecting cone that could be pushed into the fire. The rim was lipped for pouring. The cone-shaped warmer could be thrust into the heart of a barred grate fire and withdrawn by a long socket handle riveted to the rim. A variant, semicircular with a hinged lid, could be hooked with its flat side against the fire grate to keep warm after heating in the fire. This had a wooden handle, upward sloping, and a cylindrical spout.

Stills, too, may pass unrecognized although many were made in copper from the 1600s until licensing was required from 1780. By the 1770s many coppersmiths were taking advantage of the general trend towards specialization and buying factory-shaped hollow blanks stamped by drop hammer. A late 18th century coppersmith's catalogue included coach and foot warmers, water ewers and basins, pudding pans, stewpans, dairy pails, cullenders, drinking cans, tea kettles, egg poachers, flour and pepper boxes, chestnut roasters, charcoal braziers, wine strainers, cheese trays, coffee and chocolate pots with handles of black-stained boxwood and much else besides. For hollow-ware the coppersmiths might shape the ductile metal by spinning on the lathe and though the purpose was to produce light-weight cheap vessels few would deny the attraction of, for example, a spun copper teapot.

To many of us copper ware is epitomized in the glowing splendour of the copper urn. Most of these appear to be 19th century pieces made after about 1820 when copper was no longer in demand for war purposes. Some are still to be found in the inns and taverns where they were required originally to keep on tap a supply of hot water for making toddy or to keep coffee hot lest it suffer the ruination of re-heating.

Splendid copper urns were raised from the plate, like similar vessels in the silvered copper known as Sheffield plate. Design followed somewhat belatedly in the wake of late 18th century neo-classicism, Regency severity and the florid extravagance of post-Regency exuberance, con-trolled, fortunately, by the vessel's basic usefulness. The urn was evolved from the mid-18th century hot-water kettle with a tap set low in the body for replenishing the teapot. This tea-time urn was comparatively small and easy to design in accordance with current classic ideas of a wide-shouldered tapering body on a short stem and square foot. If the tap or cock projecting horizontally appears to detract from the outline it must be remembered that originally the hostess would have this for convenience pointing towards her while the urn outline unimpaired would be presented to her guests.

By the time this design spread from silver to Sheffield plate and thence to copper in the late Regency the clear, classic lines were becoming blurred. Often the shape is extremely pleasing, however, the ornament restricted to light-catching gadrooning on rim and foot, before the development of more fussy foliated detail for handles, lid and stand. An occasional footed example has been noted with motifs in the Egyptian manner and in the broad shapely lines of Paul Storr silver.

Later the taller vase shape showed attractive detail in lid finial and the like with a small tap that proved more graceful than efficient, so that in some instances this has been replaced by a single-piece casting. The usual form of tap was turned on by drawing forward a shapely bow arching over the delicate, fluted spout. Quart, 3-pint and gallon urns were made in the 18th century; the huge vessels holding 5 to 8 gallons date no earlier than about 1805.

Urn heating soon developed from the early charcoal brazier to the cylindrical box iron usually found in the copper urn. This was patented by John Wadham in 1774. The iron was made red hot in the kitchen fire and placed in a deep socket in the centre of the urn. This would maintain the heat of water or coffee poured in boiling hot. It became widely popular after the patent expired in 1788. These box heaters were so safe and simple that they were included in urn design long after lamp heaters and slow-burning mortar candles proved successful alternatives, and even when the expensive smokeless spirits of wine was replaced in the 1830s by cheaper mineral fuels. Spirit lamps, too, were improved upon from time to time through the 19th century, including attractive specimens in copper; occasionally patented designs turn up that can be dated.

On the fire itself the early brass gridiron was improved in the late 18th century by a version with crossbars grooved to drain the meat juices into a trough at the base that was spouted for emptying at one side—assuredly the kind of device to be expected of this period. But some of the most interesting brass equipment is associated with the barred coal-burning grate of the Georgian living room. The typical mid-Georgian fender of burnished steel was copied in press cut steel and then in brass sheet and by Regency days grate and fender might both be of brass, heavily cast and chased.

The old kitchen trivet was variously developed in comparable style: its popularity is shown by its eventual range of homely names—muffin stand, footman, jonathan. Brodie & Williams in 1767 patented "a rest or footman to put the kettle on", but many specimens that remain date to the early 19th century. Dickens, delighting in the warmth and colour of the fireside, makes several references—in *Martin Chuzzlewit*, for instance—to the face of the brass footman. Bob Sawyer's "right as a trivet, sir," harks back to the early advantage of a three-legged piece of furniture to stand firmly in cluttered hearth or crumbling embers, but by then the alternative phrase was "bright as a trivet", implying well-polished brass. The footman was most simply shaped as a flat iron plate supported by a pair of front legs in latten linked by a front apron decoratively pierced and supported at the back by iron rods.

Simple trivets in cast brass date mainly from the 1760s onwards. Typically the plate was of openwork with two plain straight legs at the back and one decorative brass leg at the front. A spike extending outward from the plate supported a hard wood handle for removing the hot trivet when required. Another popular design hooked to the top bar of the grate instead of resting on legs. In cast brass with openwork designs they were made from the 1770s but are rare today.

Fender trivets are to be noted, too, in cast brass for holding more vulnerable pottery teapots and muffin dishes. Basic design consisted of a round openwork plate hooked inside the fender and steadied by a single leg from its rim. The cat in brass or iron or wood was an 18th-century development of the trivet for standing inside the fender. This may be described as more or less a double tripod with six legs radiating from a central boss so that it would always stand steadily whatever way it might be placed in the hearth, like a cat that always lands on its feet. In 1806 *The Annual Register* noted a toast stand as an improvement on "those articles called cats or dogs".

Remaining copper scuttles for coal are usually late 19th-century pieces in the familiar scoop and helmet outlines. Plainer vessels were adequate when some minor servant or skivvy had to bring the coal from the back regions every time the fire burnt low. Nevertheless, as early as 1715 the very practical Lady Grisell Baillie recorded in her household accounts the buying of one for half a crown: probably she preferred to keep her servants more constructively employed. Today many people use the straightsided bucket that once belonged to the dairy.

One of the most attractive pieces of household equipment, where the bright glow of the metal served to emphasize its warmth-providing purpose, was the warming pan—all too familiar now as a thin, shoddy reproduction that could never have served to carry glowing smokeless court charcoals around the house, to take the chill from linen sheets by being passed briefly between them by an ever-watchful chambermaid. Elizabeth I in 1582 received a small warming pan of gold garnished with small diamonds and rubies. In less exalted households the warming pan of brass gradually acquired some importance. They became comparatively numerous and easy to handle during the 17th century, designed, according to Randle Holme, "to receive either hot coals [charcoal] or an iron heater in to it, which being shut close with a cover for the purpose, the maid warms her master's bed".

The warming pan handle might be solid cast and turned brass with knop ornament but more usually was a thin tapering iron, with a loop on the end for hanging on the wall. As an alternative in the second half of the century the handle might be in the Continental style with two lengths of iron linked and ended with cast and turned brass mountings. In the later years of the century more were of oak, unstained but often carved with flutes below the knop finial. To the handle shoulder was riveted a ring of metal supporting the ember pan by its flat rim. A substantial hinge joined the shoulder of the handle to the underside of the lid which in an early specimen was slightly convex, hand raised from a thin sheet of Dutch or Flemish metal. Some have been noted with attractive embossed ornament such as a coat of arms as well as a circle of holes to release the heat. Simple ornament was applied with a series of punches, although often now referred to as engraving.

The ember pan would be made of cheaper English brass. The brass ingots were hammered into sheets by the water-driven battery process and discs cut from the sheet were suitably heated and worked upon with smaller hammers until "raised" to the shape required. Hammer marks were removed on the lathe and the parts of the pan might be sold to small masters for assembly and finishing. From the 1660s the arrival of many Dutch workmen resulted in more ambitious brasswork. So far as the warming pan was concerned this meant that the lid became more convex and sometimes elaborately pierced and fret-cut with pictorial motifs, and from the 1670s it was most usually finished with a wide rim fitting on to the rim of the ember pan.

The massive ember pan of this period had straight, almost vertical, sides about $3\frac{1}{2}$ inches deep and $10\frac{1}{2}$ inches across to the edge of the rim, which was riveted to the iron ring—a flat rim about an inch wide, until someone thought of bending it down to hide the ring. A circle of iron wire might strengthen the rim of the lid.

Far more warming pans, however, date from the 1720s onwards. The whole design was then lighter in weight, with a wooden handle, and the lid extended considerably beyond the rim of the ember pan. Only in this later group can one find warming pans of copper, when there was no longer the fear that the metal might split. These were produced in four sizes between $12\frac{1}{2}$ and $10\frac{1}{2}$ inches across. The ember pan was lighter, in some $\frac{1}{16}$ inch section, the lid plain or sparsely engraved, since the perforations suited to the earlier heavy pans were no longer needed to let out the heat and the less welcome staining fumes.

This was the lid one tends to expect upon a warming pan, in the familiar beefeater hat shape with a narrow sloping rim fitting the beaded rim of the pan and with a brass ring for opening—sometimes now on a three-joint hinge, although the stronger five-lug was preferred. A tapering brass socket attached to the ember pan held the polished beech or ash wood handle. The final later 18th-century development was the pan and lid shaped in the copper by stamping and both shallower than before, with a less angular outline. In this the lid fitted inside the rim of the ember pan and the handle might be japanned.

A rarity recorded at Anne of Cleves House, Lewes, is a

bed cradle, an openwork frame surrounding a court charcoal brazier that could be left in the bed to give it a thorough airing. But the obvious dangers of live charcoals glowing among the bedclothes were eventually banished when warming pans of pewter and of copper were made instead to hold boiling water. These were introduced early in George III's reign and by 1807 Edward Thomason, a warming pan maker, was able to note that few of the charcoal type could then be sold. Of the hot-water pans the most usual has a brass cap in the centre for filling, but the most attractive has no visible opening, nothing to mar the smooth face of polished copper, being filled by unscrewing the handle.

Minor brass ware that sometimes turns up but may escape identification includes a range of muff warmers and warming boxes, variously designed to contain heated box irons. A more ingenious and heat-maintaining but dangerous alternative was the ball perforated in an elaborate pattern to release heat from a central lamp slung so that, in theory at least, it would always remain right way up.

A standing iron is an attractive little tool that is not always recognized. This consists of a ball shape upon a stem and foot which of necessity had to be substantial and therefore was given the consideration of attractive design. When the top was hot it was used for pressing rounded shapes such as caps and gathered sleeves. For essential spotless cleanliness the best of these had brass cases for the fire-heated irons. Such a survey of the brass and copper that responded to the flicker of warm firelight must leave unrecorded many another use for these endearing metals. Even for quelling an unwanted conflagration the brass worker produced what were listed in every sizeable Georgian home as "brass squirts serving in peril of fire".

Chapter Fifteen

ORNAMENTAL BRASS

ENGLISH brassmen's confidence in their material and methods in early Georgian days prompted them to introduce many delightful little articles in designs that became traditional. These are collected today mainly for their decorative value but all save the latest were made for work. Bellfounding was a complicated craft but in the 1720s hand-bells were more simply made of brass and often gilded to suggest the gleam of coveted gilded silver. They were popular for summoning servants about the house and themselves prove companionable little servants in children's bedrooms still. The full-skirted woman, hands clasped over her apron, is probably the most widely reproduced. A plain bell may measure as much as 7 inches across the mouth, its handle turned in ivory, bone or box-wood.

Other highly ornamental brasses that can still be put to a purpose are found among door stops—door porters to our word-corrupting forebears. These of course were never intended for the windswept cottage that might most need such service but to counteract the ingenuity of John Izon and Thomas Whitehurst when they devised a self-closing door mechanism in 1775. At first the porter was just a solid little ornament cast in the round and lifted by a long handle with a loop at the top or a solid finial such as the pineapple motif of hospitality. But from the 1790s the design was improved into the practical flat-back or hollow-back casting more usually found today.

The long-handled bell shape sliced in half vertically was an uninteresting design, not improved by being mounted on a lion paw in the Regency fashion. But some of these patterns are particularly attractive since they gave the brass-

31. A coppersmith's shop window, one of a street of shop fronts brilliantly displayed at the Castle Museum, York. Specimens shown here include tea and coffee pots, urns, jugs, saucepans, jelly moulds—a fascinating survey of the craftsman's wares from still to loving cup.

32. Hearthside comfort. The trivet (*upper left*) is of the simplest design and could be used with a down-hearth; it is also found with a sideways projecting handle. For placing close against the raised grate the four-legged design became popular (*upper right*) described in a patent of 1767 as "a footman to put the kettle on". *Below:* a more elaborate version of the footman with a lower shelf and with top and apron front elaborately pierced and engraved in designs that include acorns and shamrock, suggesting popular commemoration of the 1801 Union of Great Britain and Ireland.

admiring Regency excellent opportunities to introduce bold neo-classic motifs at their most beguiling. Inevitably there are plenty of lion paws supporting acanthus leaves but more imaginative designs include sphinx and winged chimera. With the queer insistence one sometimes finds in a briefly fashionable notion the door porter shared with furniture and other products of its day a liking for handles simulating twisted rope, probably of Trafalgar vintage.

Soon, however, as with mantelshelf ornament, the range of subjects became less ambitious and more homely—greyhounds and horses of the sporting 1820s and 1830s, early Victorian baskets of flowers, the inevitable bird and snake motif that cropped up time and again around 1860, the bird's upraised wings supporting the lifting ring. Swans conveniently arched for lifting were obvious subjects and there was, too, the long-necked fable figure of a bird with its head in a pitcher, the design suggesting a crane rather than Aesop's crow.

The liveliest of these guards were the celebrity figures. The only requirement, it seems, was easy recognition and the long fashion for these castings is indicated by many of the subjects, the Duke of Wellington being joined by popular Boer War generals, and early models of Punch and Judy by the seated figure of Punch long familiar from that journal's cover design created by Doyle in 1849 and still a favourite product today. Ally Sloper originated no earlier than the 1870s.

The most attractive porter castings are of brass but many more are of iron, testifying to the success of the malleable cast iron invented in 1804 that could be used for small castings with little fear of cracking. Coalbrookdale ironworks, for example, won a high reputation from 1839 for their well-finished castings, showing several at the 1851 Exhibition. Their armoured knight under a Gothic canopy has reappeared in modern copies. Uniformed soldiers were made for similar sentinel duties and look especially splendid when richly painted. An iron porter may be found with a brass lifting handle and sometimes the whole surface of the figure was originally bronzed. Another attractive notion along these lines is the iron shoe scraper, perhaps at its least appropriate and most popular when shaped as a lyre.

I have written before of the hooligan sport of knocker wrenching in the 18th century when the door rapper pivoted from loops in the escutcheon or back-plate and could be torn out, leaving the plate itself still bolted to the door. The solution to this was to drill eyes in the rapper and let it swing from a bar strongly riveted into the back-plate. But those who seek door knockers of brass will find few that date earlier than Regency days—and here too the fascinating designs of this period are now being produced from some of the old moulds.

The commonest perhaps is the lion head with a ring rapper but there are Medusa and classical female heads, there are Egyptian heads with lyre rappers and various vase and acanthus patterns including the popular hand holding a wreath. Around 1850 there was a fashion for giving the knocker a protective covering with lacquer which included saffron in the recipe and gave the brass a hint of gold: colourless lacquers date only to the 20th century.

In ornamental brasswork too it is difficult for collectors to restrict their choice to the brass and copper a cottager might have owned as well as coveted but there is a sturdy worka-day air to certain particularly collectable table snuff boxes, and to some pocket ones too, made in heavy brass and copper. These date to late Georgian and early Victorian days although some have been copied in light-weight present day brass of somewhat richer tone. Their interest lies in the combination lock mechanism that secures the lid, a simple but appealing marvel to the under-educated cottager and some protection at least against the pilfering that soon emptied the table snuff box in common use.

Their story is interesting and little known. Prescot in Lancashire had a proud reputation for inexpensive watches produced by dividing the craft among various specialists. When first France from 1810 and then America introduced cost-reducing methods of mechanical mass production the Prescot men cast around for other uses for their skills and equipment. The snuff boxes they produced in heavy brass and copper plate could be opened and closed hundreds of times a day without warping or leaking. The hinge was strong, the mechanism of the lock protected from the clogging powder by a plate of brass or iron, solder sealed, and the whole interior heavily tinned to preserve its delicate aroma. But the novelty that makes them interesting to collect today lies in the Prescot men's ingenious adaptation of their watch-making skills. The most usual of these combination locks was controlled by setting the pointers on two numbered watch dials crudely engraved upon the lid. When the pointers were turned to the correct "time" the box's catch fastener could be released. Sometimes a third control was added, the pointer shaped as a twelve-rayed sun while the sliding catch that opened the lid was often shaped as a crescent or half moon. The faces on sun and moon are crude enough but among the pocket specimens especially there is an appealing individualistic air to their decoration. To avoid accidents in the pocket the lid mechanism might be modified, the cloth-catching pointers being replaced by lines upon circular revolving studs.

Ornament on these boxes might be punched or wriggled or line engraved, ranging from scrollwork to sporting scenes and often including the owner's name or initials. The watch theme might be carried into the box's general out-line, shaped as a large watch case with curved sides, a convex lid and a circular bow above the hinge for hanging. Other boxes are in the shuttle shape that had been popular in silver around the end of the 18th century. But some are memorial pieces inscribed and carried instead of the more familiar memorial or mourning rings and these may declare their purpose by being shaped as coffins. Sometimes the lid covers sides and base hollowed out of wood and the engraving may include the name, date of death, an appropriate text and an "all-seeing eye". The majority of these ingenious boxes are plain, however, of highly burnished brass or a more golden toned alloy.

Snuff proved such a tempting extravagance that the thrifty sought means to check what they could not wholly abandon. Another type of brass snuff box with an ingenious though simpler opening device came on to the market to meet their needs and this too is now collected by those with a liking for workaday brasses and for the simple glimpses into their owners' workaday lives conveyed by names, dates and ill-spelt inscriptions.

The notion here was to limit the amount of snuff a man could take when he applied finger and thumb to the opened box, for instead of a hinged lid the opening consisted of a hole shaped like a wide-waisted figure eight, permitting no more than a small pinch with the tip of thumb and finger. The brass top and bottom of the box were screwed or riveted to the sides which consisted of a single ring of wood, circular, square, eight-sided or the like and occasionally made to suggest a brass-bound book—often red-stained boxwood or tough lignum vitae. The top of the box with its finger-and-thumb hole was covered with a second sheet of metal, circular and a little smaller, attached to it by a central pivot and cut with a corresponding hole so that, with the aid of a small stud, the user could swivel it round until the holes coincided. Often engraving on part of the lower cover was revealed only when the holes were diametrically opposed and the box therefore most securely closed. Since there was no hinged lid the box could only be filled, too, by the double hole: it was customary originally for the table snuffbox to have a small spoon for filling pocket boxes.

Numbers sometimes stamped on the underside of these brass and copper snuffboxes may cause confusion. They have been noted ranging from the 1500s to the 1900s and may be taken for manufacturing dates. In fact they show a maker's adherence to the old watchmaking tradition of consecutively numbering his products.

Ornaments as such with no purpose at all save to please the possessor meant little to workaday folk until the 19th century. Then even people with very small incomes acquired a liking for the sheer extravagant indulgence of finding each other beguiling and often naïve little gifts. Those in brass were made by men who expected their goods to stand up to hard wear but remaining specimens must usually be classed still as curios—just too recent to be antiques. Some, such as figures of Napoleon, seldom have more than souvenir value. The quality and colour of the brass and the general finish must be the collector's guide.

33: Copper urns in dark, glowing metal. *Left*: in shouldered vase outline with gadrooned ornament as favoured in late Georgian design. *Right*: somewhat later and showing swan motifs appropriate to its continuing use in a lakeside hotel. A book of the period, *The Housemaid*, stresses that the water must be put into the urns straight from the boiling kettle and the heat maintained by inserting a central box iron which is red hot from the kitchen fire.

34. Warming pans in a range of shapes and treatments easily distinguished from modern reproductions. *Left*: brass of about 1670, the lid pierced in the Continental manner and with brass-mounted iron handle. *Left centre*: two of copper from the late 18th century with machine-stamped ember pans, cast brass ferrules and beechwood handles. *Right centre*: another of the late 18th century, the polished steel lid pierced by hand-press, and one in early 18th-century copper with plain out-sloping lid and tubular iron handle. *Right*: of copper, 18th century, with hand-raised lid fitting closely inside the pan.

It is amusing to try to collect an associated pair of these ornaments, the essential requirement of those that really graced the Victorian parlour mantelshelf, such as the pelican and peacock that wished good luck to the early Victorian mother-to-be. Many were even more orthodox such as lions, wheatsheaves and the endlessly popular stag and whippet. Some of the most attractive are the miniature chairs and tables, grates, fire shovels and trivets, but only long browsing among authenticated specimens will safeguard the newcomer to these "toys" from modern issues of traditional designs.

An interesting little commentary on this trade is to be found in *Hogg's Instructor*, 1852. A maker of such goods, then classed as toymaker, when interviewed declared: "I make chiefly copper tea-kettles, coffee-pots, coal scuttles, warming pans and brass scales; these are the most run to, but I make, besides, brass and copper hammers, sandpans, fish kettles, stew-pans and other things . . . There are sixteen pieces in one copper kettle: first the handle, which has three pieces, seven in the top and cover, one for the side, two in the spout, one for the bottom and two rivets to fit the handle. They are all fit to boil water in, or cook anything you like, any one of them. You can make broth in them." This maker turned out an average of 4,992 tea kettles a year and they retailed at sixpence each.

At the 1851 Exhibition a prize medal was awarded for "kitchen utensils &c made of copper, most beautifully finished" and comment was made upon the collection of miniature kitchen utensils in tinned iron plate, sold in sets for 6s. 8d. and "much used as chimney ornaments". Glass and pewter were put to this purpose too but none could compete with the sparkle of copper and brass.

Most dangerous of all to the tyro collector perhaps are horse brasses. The right ones have a mellow sheen about them that is understandably irresistible but far more are merely cheap little castings poorly finished and given inappropriate signs of "wear". So many of those found today have been made as souvenirs, so many more as deliberate imitations or fakes that there is a danger that all will be dismissed as olde worlde nonsense. This will be a real loss for here is a small but lively contribution to men's view of a way of life, recent yet utterly remote.

The souvenirs find a place among commemorative curios but alarmingly abundant fakes multiply daily for quick sale to collectors who have never even seen a horse dressed in the finery that was the pride of the mid-Victorian wagoner and drayman. This perhaps is the first point for the would-be collector to realize. The genuine horse brasses collected today date almost wholly from Victoria's reign and the majority to the 1860s–90s with all that this implies regarding quality of metal, methods of production and care of finish—and evidence of both their proud use and their laborious maintenance.

Ever since the driven horse became one of man's most important—and vulnerable—sources of livelihood attempts have been made to protect it from more than the common equine ailments. The Romans determined to ward off the evil eye by dazzling it with bright discs of bronze that would flash and twinkle distractingly with the horse's every movement. Small amulets of this kind, domed and ridged to scatter their darts of light, have been found among horse trappings dating to the days of Roman Britain, and the Roman notion of parading their driven horses in such eye-catching splendour on occasions of festival has persisted into our own times in county show and May Day parade.

Records of ceremonial occasions through Stuart and Georgian days show many a carriage horse wearing amulets upon its harness—sun, heart, crescent moon, fleur-de-lis. The face-piece worn upon its forehead was an 18th-century notion as a domed, flat-rimmed disc. This became a sun in the 19th century, with serrated edge from the 1820s, then with perforated rays and later still with drilled perforations around the rim until by the 1880s an ornament that had begun as a massive piece of latten plate was being stamped, dome and all, from thin rolled brass. Some of the most interesting of these contain central mounts of coloured glass or china and date to the 1890s.

Occasionally one comes across a fly terret or swinger, a ring to be placed upright on the horse's head to support a small brass which could therefore be shaped in the round, as a brewer's barrel perhaps or a tinkling bell. Or one may find—but rarely—a set of bells arranged in rows with great care for the harmony of their music and intended for the horse's collar. In Sussex such bells in a frame were known as rumblers, their purpose being to announce a wagon's passage along a narrow lane so that an approaching vehicle might wait in a passing place since backing a wagon with a team of horses would be a nightmare undertaking.

A wide, more or less rectangular brass sometimes turns up, a name plate intended to be used with the piece of curbing harness known as a hame. But for the most part the brasses to look for are more or less circular discs with shouldered loops for the leather straps that suspended them from the driven horse's martingale—the wide strap passing from the nose band or reins to the girth. These brasses were introduced little earlier than 1830 and the collector may expect to find their brass to be of the good quality and high finish then required of the makers of horse "furniture". Few can be identified exactly but the collector is always on the watch for a chance name or date.

A valuable rarity is a set of brasses on its original martingale—of horsehide or rarer hogskin or of cowhide worn and polished to pliant texture and mellow tone far different from modern leather. Such a set may include the harness supplier's name on the lowest brass or a date of purchase engraved or punched on its frame. A horse brass displaying the royal crown is another occasional find, probably sold at some time as surplus by the Office of Works from the Royal Mews or one of the Ministries: early ones show the crown cast in relief and brazed into a frame; later ones stamped shaping. Very occasionally too one finds a brass with the diamond-shaped Registration mark on the back used between 1842 and 1883 to prevent copying of a design (see Chapter Twelve).

The most ambitious style of identifiable horse brass, however, was the face-piece with an estate crest: heraldic brasses for the saddlery trade were shown at the 1851 Exhibition including specimens in costly prince's metal finished by gilding; others were cast in silver-toned alloy and silver plated. But today even the brass with a horse's name upon it is an exception. The majority offer only subtler clues in the nature of their ornament—the Sussex wagoner with his whip, the Staffordshire knot, the windmill popular in windswept Lincolnshire, the shepherd and windmill motif made for a prosperous Walsall horse dealer in the 1870s–90s, the phoenix used by the Phoenix Brewery of that period, the rearing horse of Kent.

Since all these brasses were for driven horses in public view motifs such as plough and cow immediately declare themselves as very late on the scene when designs tended to be indiscriminate. Railway locomotives on brasses may be identified by the specialist, being found in more than twenty patterns, some tracing their development from the "Rocket" onwards. Railway company monograms and initials are easier for the rest of us. All date to the years when massive horses pulling delivery drays clattered splendidly over the cobbles of every station yard.

In these and in innumerable other patterns collectors must decide the date of manufacture for themselves. Early brasses pre-dating about 1860 are hard to find anyway but those who can pick out the old brass containing calamine, hand-worked or cast (see Chapter Thirteen), can escape the risk of modern reproductions. A few of the finest were cast in a high-quality brass of the prince's metal type and others appear notably smooth and clear-cut in the golden spelter brass as it was first evolved by James Emerson. Others of these early brasses were made in the cheaper calamine brass but specially treated to acquire a golden tone and further enlivened with touches of burnishing. But most of the genuine brasses found today date to 1860 and later. Spelter brass was then in more general use, at first for solid little castings and from the 1870s for lighter but less individualistic machine stampings in the rolled sheet, finished at first by careful hand-filing.

The early suns, stars, crescents were then rivalled by a great range of more interesting motifs. These castings were given a scrupulous hand-finish that puts to shame the modern fake cast in common industrial brassfounders' metal and with the mould projections known as gets often left unfiled. A catalogue of the 1880s included 300 numbered patterns. Horses, horseshoes, sporting animals are obvious subjects, though the pendant horse as an unframed relief casting is usually a 20th-century creation. Some attractive pelicans and peacocks are found, the bird cast in the round and brazed into a separately cast frame, a style adapted to a wide range of motifs from wheatsheaf to thistle flower. These are very different pieces of work from many of the swans, lyre-birds, turkeys and other comparatively modern single-piece castings. Acorns and oak leaves are found as castings too, often crescent-framed and dating to the late 19th century.

Many of the stamped brasses dating from the 1870s onwards resemble earlier castings but are light little pieces made even lighter by elaborate perforations and with the relief parts showing hollow on the reverse. Simpler stamped motifs include hearts, playing card suits, scallop shells and formal patterns of perforations.

In contrast the elaborate portrait brasses are mainly 20th-century souvenirs. The early "bun" profile of Queen Victoria is a rarity now but three-quarter and full-face portraits made for the 1887 and 1897 jubilees are fairly numerous. Early Prince of Wales feathers may be found but more of recent origin and there are portraits of Edward VII before and after he became king.

Other late-19th-century brasses commemorate Gladstone, for instance, and Randolph Churchill and Disraeli wreathed in primroses. These were followed early this century by Shakespeare, Wesley, Nelson, Kitchener, even Sir Winston Churchill and Viscount Montgomery. R.S.P.C.A. "merit badges" date from 1896 onwards and their shield-shaped brasses from 1902 when the public as well as the stableman was aware that more than good luck emblems and the dazzle of well-polished brasswork was needed to do justice to the splendour of the shire horse between the shafts.

Chapter Sixteen

COTTAGE LIGHTING

BRASS in all its varying tones and qualities down the ages has always most nearly approached the splendour of gold when lit by the mellow glow of candles. The Stuart, Georgian, even Victorian cottage dweller depended mainly on iron for his lighting equipment. Householders with more money to spare might seek to suggest the cool gleam of silver by buying candlesticks of 17th-century pewter, perhaps, or 18th-century snuffers of burnished steel or a Regency wax jack of Sheffield plate. Nevertheless, cottage dwellers today look for brass candlesticks and they must have been doubly precious when catching a lovely twinkle from the cheap, unmannerly kinds of candle suffered in everyday use until little more than a hundred years ago.

Brass candlesticks stood midway between the craftsman's superb silver and the blacksmith's tough iron, showing some of the best qualities of each. Candles themselves have improved almost ou of recognition. Sweet candles of bees-wax were party luxuries and the majority were of tallow either dipped or shaped in tapering moulds around wicks of cotton, flax, sometimes the pith of rushes. Even the best wicks required frequent snuffing until early Victorian days. Now snuffers and their stands are reduced to the status of decorative idlers. But candlesticks in service through the past couple of centuries retain their simple usefulness to this day.

As brass making in England improved around the begin-ning of the 18th century, candlestick styles changed in step with fashion. Throughout the collector's period from the beginning of the 18th century they closely followed the patterns established by silver. Inevitably this has meant the introduction of recent copies in particularly desirable shapes and patterns so that the collector has to rely upon a shrewd eye for the colour, texture and finish of the brass when hunting out the real antique.

In the rare specimen from the 17th century the outline may recall the wood turner's repetitive ball or bead outline on the tall socket above the wide flange and on the short body below that spreads into a domed foot. Towards the end of the century the grease pan might be omitted, letting the guttering candlewax spill down the plain or pillar stem into a saucer-shaped base. In unamenable early English brass the stick was cast in a solid piece and finished by lathe turning and drilling. But with the more malleable brass of the early 18th century came the stick cast in two halves, vertically seamed and mounted on a solid cast base.

Handsome socketed candlesticks in silver style were then developed, but for everyday use the old styles were long continued. The straight stem was made more practical, too, by providing a slide inside that could raise the candle as required and get rid of the burnt-down end. The most usual lift has a decorative thumb piece and works in a vertical slot with a series of side notches. This meant that the candle need never project far above the flanged nozzle and was so practical that it was never really outmoded in kitchen or cottage despite fashion's change to shallow sockets with removable nozzles.

These early 18th-century socketed candlesticks are some of the most attractive ever made and well deserved their return to fashion a century later. They were given the baluster and acorn knop stems of silver and their response to the flickering candlelight might be enhanced by gadrooning and the rounded outlines of moulding where the socket joined the stem. The foot might be highly domed or deeply concave.

Early Georgian metalwork design welcomed the sparkle of candlelight with faceted stems and sharp-cornered octagonal sockets and feet. But all too soon brass followed silver into lobed outlines, the shouldered or silesian stem being set on a foot, four-lobed at first, then six-lobed, and by the mid-century shaped into a series of shallow, characterless scallops.

The tiny seam marks could be avoided from the 1770s

when socket and stem were shaped as a single hollow casting: this may be regarded as the third stage in the development of brass candlesticks. A rod pushed up through the hollow casting ejected the candle end, doing away with the need for slide and slot. It is well to note that the candlestick cast as a single piece, socket stem and foot, was a mid-Victorian development: so much for the authenticity of many a specimen sold as antique today.

Early chandeliers and simpler multi-socket candle beams might be of brass or latten. Rare remaining specimens date to Stuart days. Sconces, too, were made in brass and were so attractive that one can only wish they had stayed longer in fashion. A typical specimen of the early 1700s in the Victoria and Albert Museum has an S-shaped branch curving out from the gadrooned base of the brass escutcheon so that the candle beam would reflect directly on its polished central shield and twinkle from the surrounding leaf scrolls where different qualities of matting would give a mellow tone and reduce dazzle.

Brassfounders' catalogues through the 18th and early 19th centuries show a continuing interest in brass candle branches, plain and with an abundance of foliate ornament, but these lack the earlier reflective sconces, being intended either to fit directly to the wall in a flurry of rococo scrollwork or to use with mirror glass in carved and gilded frames. The Regency's eagle-surmounted circular convex mirror was often enriched with candle branches and sometimes one finds elaborations of brasswork replacing the mirror, or wall branches hung with the early 19th century's well-loved "icicles" or faceted lustres, popular in the parlour but appearing ill at ease in a cottage setting today.

In Britain especially candles of wax and tallow continued to be the most usual forms of lighting in all but the poorest homes throughout the 18th and early 19th centuries. Attractive candlesticks in neo-classic style date from the 1760s onwards. This is the familiar shape with a tall tapering stem, often square in section and on a square base such as a substantial stepped plinth. The foot developed a moulded edge in the mid-1760s and the rarer gadrooned edge in the 1770s. For the last twenty years of the century the socket

35. Lancashire snuffboxes with ingenious fasteners that may go unrecognized among brass and copper curios. *Top left:* table specimen in copper, its crescent moon slide-latch released by correct setting of the three revolving studs. *Top right:* pocket specimen secured by revolving pointers. *Centre left and right:* hardwood boxes with only finger-tip openings, that on the left a *memento mori* dated 1847. *Bottom left:* shuttle shape in copper with bright-cut engraving and owner's initials. *Bottom right:* watch shape, the moon latch released by two dial pointers and a twelve-rayed sun.

36. Horse brasses. At top are two hame plates. The central martingale shows sun, crescent and perforated patterns topped by the harness maker's name, Wilkinson of Whitehaven. To the sides are playing-card motifs and lower right a loin strap including small brasses for individual inscriptions.

was a wide-rimmed vase shape often partly gadrooned, the stem most often fluted, square or round in section and tapering from a wide shoulder to end in a high pyramid or domed foot. This style was still popular in the mid-19th century.

As explained in an earlier chapter, some of the finest of these candlesticks were made in the lovely golden brass evolved by Emerson in 1770, their cast ornament clear and unpitted, their surfaces burnished. But the period produced, too, its quota of simple cut-price sticks in the cheaper calamine brass. Loose nozzles became usual late in the 18th century. The early 19th century reintroduced many an old familiar style of stick with a socket, stem and foot in the comfortable plump baluster outlines of a century before, but differences in the ways they were made should prevent any confusion in dating. The telescopic candlestick, patented in 1796, was another long-lasting favourite. This has a rim nozzle and its straight socket and upper stem slide down into the trumpet shape of the lower section.

Chamber candlesticks became important in early Georgian days for carrying a light from room to room, the stem and socket low, the base spread into a wide dish, square or circular, to catch the inevitable trail of wax and lifted by a curled-over handle with a flat and usually well-shaped thumbpiece. This had obvious advantages over the early method of coating a tallow candle with fine wax to protect the fingers from its clinging odour when it was carried through the house. The stem was equipped with a slide for ejecting the candle end and the handle with a projection for an extinguisher.

The tubular chamber stick with a tall protective glass was an important late 18th-century development and the brass man made use of his opportunity for decoration in the piercings around the base. The most familiar 19th-century version of this draught-protected style has a wide central socket, perforated at the base and mounted on a dish with a side handle. To be complete there should be an extinguisher with a long handle from its cone tip for the user to reach the candle without moving the hot glass.

The most useful style of chamber candlestick, and now a

prize indeed when found complete, had not only an extinguisher hooked to the curl of the handle but a pair of snuffers tucked through a slit in the stem below the socket. An early 19th-century catalogue illustrated decorated chamber candlesticks in bronze costing from 5s. 10d. to 10s. 6d. a pair and "if with bronzed snuffers, 2/6d pr. extra".

Scissor-like snuffers share the candle's long history, since the early candle wick required frequent trimming to ensure a clear flame. Yet all that is now so utterly a part of a vanished ritual that it may be well to recall that it was a task every house servant had to learn: a large establishment would employ a boy solely to cope with the innumerable flickering, guttering, flaring candles and considered his tiny wage well spent as he poked up curling wicks, trimmed their charred ends with his pointed scissor-like shears to encourage a clear regular flame and check the "thief in the candle".

Brass snuffers were shapely versions of his iron tool. Others again were made of steel, with silver always to set an example of well-proportioned design with an instinctive grace of line in each basically functional detail. An occasional relic of the 17th century shows the blades fitted with small boxes that closed together to make a heart shape, but an improved design soon had the box on one blade and a flat press upon the other to force the cut wick into the box and extinguish it with the minimum of smouldering.

Snuffers were attractive necessities to the Georgian. An occasional rarity is the brass snuffer of the early to mid-18th century in the silversmith's particularly attractive design with the holder resembling a wide-based baluster candlestick but with a handle shaped as a small arch or loop: this supports the snuffers vertically, finger loops upwards. But this was mainly a Continental style and in any case it was short-lived. Today it is rare enough even to find an early pair of snuffers in cast brass presented in the more customary manner, lying flat in a snuffers tray. An occasional early oval or waisted-oval tray is found with tiny feet and a handle projecting from one side, but from about the 1750s it was usual for the tray to be plain and nearly flat and for

158

the snuffers themselves to be fitted with three short feet: these raised the tool slightly above the tray so that it was the more easily lifted by its finger loops.

The box on the blade that received the cut wick was most often rectangular as in the 17th century, but might be an oval, lozenge or half globe. It continued to be an annoyance to the user until methods were devised to keep the fragments of hot wick from falling out when more than one candle was snuffed. The first of these "mechanical snuffers" was patented by Benjamin Cartwright in 1749. This contained a coiled spring to control the movement. It was followed by a number of further patents which by their claims indicate that the difficulty was not easily overcome. An early Victorian book of instructions, *The Housemaid* stresses that candles must be lifted off the dinner table for snuffing lest any snuff fall in the food.

For a time a design with a barrel-shaped wick box was particularly popular. But the enthusiast can find quite a range of early 19th-century notions to meet the problem. In 1810, for example, Samuel Hobday of Birmingham introduced a concealed lever that automatically raised and dropped the shutter as the wick was cut, and he drew attention to the fact with the words "without spring" upon the tool. Eight years later he improved on this with a snuffer without a lever either.

Henry Shrapnell devised an arrangement of spikes in the back of the wick box patented in 1837 and the period's unbounding ingenuity produced also gun trigger actions and the like. Most of these were too complicated to win much success but they persisted with patents into the 1840s until suddenly silenced by the obscure weaver's revolutionary idea for a wick that required no snuffing. This wick was plaited with one tight strand that caused it to curl into the flame as it burned and thus kept the end trimmed.

This eventually banished the snuffers to the collector's cabinet, but douters or extinguishers were still required: these have small discs instead of cutters to snuff out the flame. Occasionally a pair of snuffers included the discs as an elaboration of its projecting point, but these are rare indeed. Most people relied instead upon the simple cone extinguisher that could be pressed down upon the candle —successfully or too heavily according to the user's skill. Trays for early 19th-century snuffers included a four-lobed pattern that carried a pair of cone extinguishers. Snuffer trays for elegant households were loaded with the required rococo ornament of the 1820s-30s but cottage surroundings may more gladly welcome the brightly coloured, closely ornamented trays of papier mâché and japanned iron, popular with early Victorians and more popular than ever among the functional trimmings of today.

For outdoor use and rough work the obvious development of the chamber candlestick was the lantern widely used throughout the 18th century in the styles familiar to this day. Quality details may include traces of repoussé ornament and the essential ventilation holes saw-cut in decorative patterns. The interior was fitted with a firmly based candle socket and the vertical sides and hinged door had sheets of horn plate. Some, instead, made use of the bull's eye glass produced in the process of making window glass but discarded because of its obscuring striations and central protuberance. Small circles of glass could be fitted in a cylindrical lantern, the light released also through a pattern of perforations over the surrounding metalwork, but for a specimen of better quality the base was square and the roof a more elaborate dome. The principle was the same throughout, with a low candle-socket, a side door for access hinged and hasped, and more or less decorative ventilation louvres in the sloping roof protected against the weather. For carrying there might be a loop handle at one side or a ring in the top that could become uncomfortably warm. Folding lanterns were made for the traveller who might be late home. A typical design folded almost flat and fitted with its taper into a small pocket-flat case.

For use indoors in the 19th century away from wind a lantern might have its light protected by a window of wire gauze, but this was essentially a cheap kitchen and cellar tool. Lanterns became really handsome affairs when they were devised as fixtures for indoor passage or staircase or for outdoor yard or gateway. Some of these were fitted for oil-burning lamps.

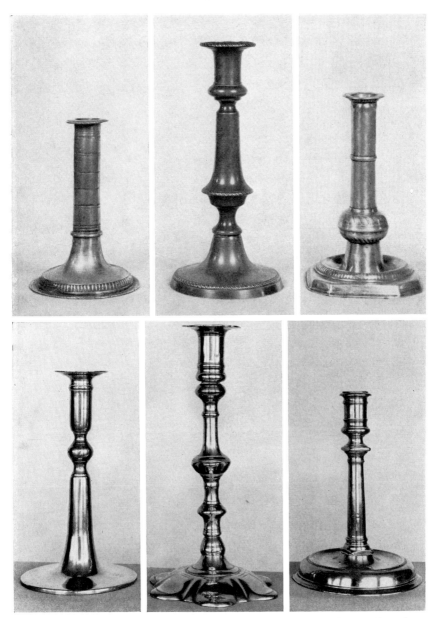

37. Candlesticks showing simplification of fashion styles into shapely but sturdy outlines.
Upper row: in pewter. The pillar designs are of the late 17th century with simple ringed and
knopped stems and with cording as a modification of fashionable gadrooning on their footrims.
In the centre the slightly sagging line characteristic of the 1830s; this is 8½ inches tall. *Below:*
the central multi-knopped specimen on the scalloped foot fashionable around the mid-18th
century is 9¾ inches tall, cast in brass. Flanking it are two of the same century cast in the related
alloy gun-metal.

38. Cottage lamps. *Top:* a spout lamp and a Betty lamp or lidded crusie. *Centre:* a more elaborate two-wick form and a hanging spout lamp in brass. *Below:* Georgian double-valve crusie and 17th-century floor standard lamp with the slightly spouted open pans that evolved from the slut.

In kitchen and workshop and throughout many a cottage the source of light was a lamp with a wick of hemp or pith or other vegetable matter burning whale or fish-liver oil. As mentioned on page 163, from 1709 to 1831 animal fats and vegetable oils were monopolized by the candlemakers. An early, simple style of lamp, messy as its name suggests, was the "slut", with a home-made wick floating in oil in an open circular bowl of iron or latten. By Stuart days this had been improved into the crusie or cresset with a part of the side pinched out into an open beak spout to support the wick. This burnt more reliably but oil dripped from the wick over the vessel's edge and before the end of the century the double crusie had been evolved, a somewhat unimaginative affair with a second identical spouted vessel under the lamp that would catch the drips. Each vessel had a vertical handle for hanging and by linking these with an arrangement of loop and ratchet the lamp could be tilted as required to feed the oil to the wick. Some were canoe-shaped, others square with protruding corners, to take two or four wicks.

From these evolved the more practical lamp with a hinged lid, but this in its turn was soon improved upon by introducing an open-channel wick holder so attached inside the lipped vessel that the oil surplus flowed back into the reservoir. In these, too, more than one wick might be burned, but it is hard indeed today to imagine how fine craftsmen tolerated their puny light, often through much of their twelve-hour working day.

The spout lamp that was developed from slut and crusie flickered and fumed in uncountable numbers of cottages and workshops from the 1720s. The little vessel, lidded and spouted, stood on a thick hollow stem with a wide foot weighted with sand. It might be in polished brass, copper or tin plate as an alternative to iron. Its circular, enclosed oil reservoir served a straight, tubular wick holder slanting forward from the base with a gutter to catch oil dripping from the wick and channel it back into use. The round plaited wick tended to crust and the lamp was incomplete without an iron wick-pick chained to the lid, but at least its light was as good as might be expected from a couple of candles.

An interesting little offshoot of this was the bedside lamp made from the late 1720s and illustrated, for example, in *The Craftsman* of 1730. This had a case of brass enclosing a tubular glass oil reservoir: as the lamp burned through the night the oil level sank and the time could be read from markings on the tube.

Early in George III's reign there was some improvement, especially in the wick, which was made as a thin ribbon, more accessible to the air, and the lamp itself was a more competent little article. Primitive as they were, lamps of this open-wick type lit many a cottage family far into the 19th century. They could serve instead of candles in shaded hanging lamps or on handled trays like chamber candlesticks. In cast brass with a neo-classic Roman air they are still to be found, but few would choose to use them.

A steadier light could be obtained with the Swiss-patented Argand lamp of the early 1780s: this had a tubular wick so that air could flow smoothly to the little ring of flame guarded within a glass chimney. The Liverpool lamp of the 1800s was a development from the Argand, with an adjustable disc set above the wick to expand the flame for greater light and with the lower part of the chimney rounded out to accommodate it. The oils available in Regency and post-Regency years still worried English lamp designers, however. The result was the typical and extremely attractive style with the brass font containing the sluggish fuel placed above the projecting burners. Grecian urn fonts were followed by the more globular Roman outlines for these fonts with appropriate classic ornament: they appeared in hanging lamps on long brass chains, on pillar-stemmed table lamps above horizontally branching lights and on wall lights supported by foliate brackets. And how the early 19th century brassfounder loved his foliate scrolls.

Somewhat pompous brass castings in the revived rococo mood appeared in the 1820s and more elaborate glass chimneys. Brassfounders' pattern books illustrate table lamps with tall fluted stems on massive pitch-weighted plinths with acanthus and lion paw detail. The collector has to realize, however, that even when one of these lamps is found its chimney is likely to be a later replacement and any pendant lustre ornament may well be suspect. In any case these lamps are not plentiful: they have long been popular collector items and doubtless, though many were made, many too were discarded during the experimental period with the explosive "burning liquids" that followed the discovery of benzine in 1825 and the subsequent development of camphene and the like. These were cleaner, cheaper, brighter than whale oil and preferred to sluggish vegetable oils but thankfully abandoned with the coming of paraffin which, in 1861, ended all demand for lamps in simple traditional style.

No survey of cottage lighting can avoid mention of the rush-light holder. Down the years this has acquired a glamour out of all proportion to its original usefulness. It appears to have come into service no earlier than the 17th century and its inadequate little light glimmered in cottage and outbuilding through the 18th and early 19th centuries simply because better alternatives were prohibited to those who had to rely on lights of their own devising. When the candle tax became law in 1709 its purpose was to ensure success to the candlemakers' trade and a licence was required costing the household a shilling per head per year even to make home scraps into candles and the same law permitted lamps only if they burnt more or less noisome, smoky fish or whale oil. This left the cottager "rushlights made at home and passed only once through grease or kitchen stuff and not at all through any tallow melted or refined".

The law was repealed in 1831 but it was later still before the rushlight was abandoned. "Rush peelers for rushlights" were noticed in 1885. When its functional but often somewhat graceless fittings are found today they may well prove to have a mid-Victorian rather than a medieval pedigree.

As late as 1673 Aubrey found it worth commenting as novel that "the people of Ockley in Surrey draw peeled rushes through melted grease, which yields a sufficient light for ordinary use, is very cheap and useful, and burns long". Splits of pinewood were preferred when available, preferably ancient wood from the bogs, as new wood had to be soaked in melted resin. Gilbert White in 1775 calculated that a rushlight burned on average for half an hour and that five-and-a-half hours of such light cost the cottager a farthing. The common soft rush was used, peeled save for a narrow rib which gave strength to the flimsy pith—two ribs for the still dimmer, slower burning "watch lights" that even White admitted gave "a dismal light".

The grease of whatever kind available was melted in a heavy iron grisset, canoe-shaped with a long handle, and the rushes passed slowly through it one by one so that the porous pith could absorb it before it cooled and solidified. Even when the grease included beeswax or mutton fat, however, the rushlight was too flimsy to stand without support. Hence the holder devised with a pair of nippers to grip it, a straight stem for varying its height and a solid base to hold it steady on the rough cottage floor.

The nippers' grip was a simple scissor cross standing vertically with one arm curving down to the main supporting rod and the other arm curving out to end in a small weight; this ensured that the rushlight, held slightly aslant, was secure without depending upon a spring. The weight might be no more than a decorative curl but was often a small candle-socket shaped as a narrow funnel. Sometimes it was a spiral of thick wire that made the most of candle scraps. Sometimes one finds a spike instead, simpler still for burning a candle end. The frugal could augment the rushlight then for essential duties but retain the small gleam when the candle was as quickly douted again.

Some simple rushlight holders of early days are pleasant little specimens of the smith's skill with wrought iron and are based for cheapness upon woodblocks, often turned with attractive mouldings. Mostly these are for table use. When an adjustable holder was required to stand on the floor beside spinning wheel or work bench the design was limited to a thin vertical rod with a small finial such as an acorn at the top and a wrought iron stop—essential for safety above a rush-strewn floor—attached near the base. Between these a slide holding the rushlight nippers could be moved to any required height and held by a friction spring. The wooden block was indication that iron was costly: when it became cheaper in the 18th century the holder's base could be a metal tripod with simple projecting feet, four-footed when used on table or well-paved floor.

A further change from the late 18th century onwards was from wrought iron to castings with all this implies in design and finish. Often the holder suggests the pillar and claw outline of contemporaneous furniture and the counterweight on the nippers arm may be a handsome little detail, but this was never an article that lent itself to prettifying. Another style of holder could be hung from the ceiling, with a ratchet to adjust its height like an adjustable pothook, and eventually it was found that a serviceable holder could be achieved with a strong spring clip on a plain rod grasping the rushlight like a pair of tweezers.

One occasional confusion is perhaps worth a final word. A coil of pliant wax-coated wick is sometimes found, and when wound upon its original little stand or curled inside an appropriately fitted box, it is a find indeed. This was a wax jack or wax taper holder, not originally a cottage piece at all but now extremely desirable. Some were of silver or Sheffield plate but brassfounders listed them in the early 19th century. The reel of pliant taper might be wound vertically or horizontally on the spindle and was topped by nippers which were widened to catch stray drips and based on a solid foot, with an upcurving handle for carrying. The result was a safe minimal light for taking about the house in days when the prospective labour of making a light must have meant that many a letter went unsealed and many a pipe unsmoked.

Chapter Seventeen

A SILLY little caricature print issued when Queen Victoria and her Consort visited Paris, shows Prince Albert, tankard in hand, attempting to persuade the French Empress "to do as we English man's do, drink out of de Pewtere!" It is curious today how hard we find it to associate this gentle-faced metal with the noisy tartans and dressy gilded china of Victorian days. Probably even among those who introduced pewter plates and mugs as the perfect companions for their lovely oak dresser racks there are many who still link all pewter only with the early history of this country when the great Pewterers' Guild rigidly controlled its manufacture.

Writers on the subject tend to dwell on the Stuart and early Georgian design and craftsmanship so widely faked in recent years and the collector finds little enough help with the genuine minor pieces that can still be identified and collected in what was first and foremost a workaday ware. Indeed, today even identification may be difficult enough. How many collectors, I wonder, know the constituents of their lustrous alloy? Certainly not the cottage woman as little as a hundred years ago, beguiled by the silver-tongued hawker at her door into buying, say, a tankard of lead filmed over with tin or a teapot with a false "loaded bottom" of a valueless filling which by its weight made her imagine that she was buying a bargain.

By then of course the hawker's intention was to trick her into thinking she was buying lead-free Britannia metal. But here again collectors tend to class all their dun-toned alloys merely as pewter without further qualification and never look for the whole intriguing story behind this appealing ware. Yet it is possible to trace the rise and fall of the pewterers, their increasing struggle against competition, and not only from such splendid wares as Sheffield plate and its successors, though this too is a story of early triumph and eventual extinction.

Just as all the heat-fused plated silver wares of Sheffield and Birmingham were gradually out-priced and out-moded by Elkington's electro-deposit silvering, so in the previous century the pewterer had lost ground as the public seized upon the next development of cheap china-bright earthenwares. But as they cut costs by adding more and more lead they had only their disorganized manufacturers to blame when they found their wares ousted by what was hailed at the time as a wonderful new white metal. This under various names has been decried by Dickens and others, the implication being that it was sham silver, testimony in itself to the ware's attractive gleam. Even some pewter collectors themselves have failed to realize that here, re-born, was pewter in the finest quality of its early heyday which could only regain acceptance in George III's reign by appearing under other names.

All this comes late in any chronological survey of pewter, but it is important, I think, to establish the basic facts before getting happily lost among the delectable items that can still be found for a cottage setting. The metals known as Roberts plate and British plate have no direct bearing upon this story; they were the obvious and important successors to silver-fused Sheffield plate. All were substitutes for solid silver, outmoded by the electro-plating that is familiar and perhaps too easily despised today as soon as a collector identifies the letters EPNS (electro-plated nickel silver) beside the maker's mark.

Entirely different in substance and purpose is the series of "white metals" that transformed current workaday pewter: these include French metal—occasionally "French pewter"—Vickers' metal, tutania, Britannia metal and variants of Britannia metal under such names as Argentine plate, queen's metal, Ashberry's metal. But it must be remembered that new pewter in any form appealed to the cottager because its bright tin, newly burnished on the lathe, looked very much like silver. Moreover, after 1820, with new manufacturing techniques, Britannia metal could forsake traditional pewter forms and be presented in all the splendour of shape and ornament then expected of silver and Sheffield plate.

Pewter under strict guild laws of the 17th century was basically a toughened tin, and tin-and-temper—more or less tin and a little brass—was long the term for finest quality pewter. Pure tin in all its bright beauty was too pliant for rough-and-tumble wear and was strengthened with a small quantity of bismuth and copper—later antimony; also, unfortunately, it could be eked out with lead. The Pewterers' Guild distinguished between fine metal and the blue-tinged ley metal that might contain up to 25 per cent. of lead.

By old tradition best-quality metal was used for the tough duties required of plates and dishes. But even this soon acquired a film of oxidization through exposure to the air and the specialists who shaped those pleasant plates were known as sad-ware men. Collectors value the tone and surface patination and are quick to note when old pewter has been melted down and recast into a less porous substance, less pleasant to the finger tips. Sometimes overdrastic cleaning with hydrochloric acid leaves an old piece with a bright but pitted surface that is puzzling, but the observant collector can usually detect the difference between a modern reproduction and the sad-ware man's plate which was shaped by casting, trimmed in the lathe and expertly hammered to harden the curve of the bouge, making the metal compact and rigid; final cleaning of the upper surface left hammer marks visible on the underside.

The name trifle was given to the quality of pewter, usually containing more antimony, required for drinking vessels; and ley metal for the heavily leaded ware shaped into such working vessels as candle moulds and the measures required for selling liquids.

Some of these measures, whatever their leaden tone, are particularly collectable. With pewter wine measures in baluster outlines, for example, it is possible to puzzle out at least half a dozen details of their construction that helped the customer to detect any attempt at reducing the measure's capacity on the part of a wily barman. The Scottish tappit hen, outward curving for the upper part of the body and nearly vertical above and below, is a familiar and delightful vessel. Its original capacity was a Scots pint, equal to three of Imperial measure, with chopin and mutchkin as bigger and smaller versions, but by the early 19th century a whole range of sizes was made from a gill to half a gallon and these are now all tappit hens to their admirers.

Eventually the blue-grey "thundercloud" tone of leaded lay metal might indicate as much as 40 per cent. of this cheaper poisonous lead in its formula and gradually such inferior short-lived vessels were all that was expected of pewter. Only as late as 1907 was the tendency checked and the allowable maximum reduced to ten per cent. of lead.

All this was understandable, of course, as the pewterers had to cut their prices in face of competition from all well-glazed earthenwares. It is interesting to note, for instance, that pewter plate rims gradually lost their elaborately reeded edges and were often merely thickened on the underside when their rivals were smooth-rimmed plates of cream ware. But as early as the mid-17th century a Frenchman, James Taudin, had been at logger-heads with the Pewterers' Guild, producing a durable pewter distinguishable by its sonorous ring, which he marked E. SONNANT. By the mid-18th century "a white hard pewter with a clear sound" was acknowledged: this might be marked with a crowned X and, more surprisingly, with such words as "Superfine French metal". This, with some modification of formula, was the high-quality descendant of "the Frenchman's pewter" and hence, to make it wholly acceptable, "French metal", occasionally found in spoons, tankards and plates of the 1770s.

Meanwhile in 1769 John Vickers of Sheffield paid five shillings for a formula for a tin alloy and was so impressed with his bargain that at once he set about manufacturing goods in "Vickers white metal", and here again the curious fact is that the ware closely resembled the fine early plate pewter of the sad-ware men. He was noted in 1787 as a maker of bits and stirrups, of measures, teapots, caster frames and salt spoons of white metal; cream jugs, sugar basins, tobacco boxes and beakers have been found too, the fine construction and careful ornament suggesting that he aimed to rival the style as well as the silver brightness of Sheffield plate. They are now rarities but can be recognized when found by the name I. VICKERS impressed in small capital letters.

Another Birmingham man, William Tutin, mixed tin and antimony in much the same way to the proportions of the old pewterers' trifle and called the white metal tutania. This sometimes gets confused with the Chinese nickel alloy tutenag—though nickel alloys are yet another theme in this unwieldy story of white metal developments and of no consequence here unless a collector is puzzled by a piece of "German silver"—a common name for a nickel alloy containing no silver. Once electro-plating had become popular in the second half of the 19th century the story of all these alloys was more or less concluded anyway, for all, Britannia metal and German silver alike, were entirely lost to view, smothered under a thin film composed of tiny particles of pure silver.

Meanwhile, through the vastly productive first half of the 19th century the important name for the pewter collector was Britannia metal. The formula of the early Vickers white metal was altered a little in the early 1790s to produce an alloy with a coarser texture, less closely resembling silver but harder and more lasting. This was composed of some ninety per cent. of tin with a trace of copper and a little of the brittle, slow-to-tarnish, bluish-white metal antimony.

The main point about this innovation—or rediscovery— was that this Britannia metal was leadless, highly lustrous, with a silvery white tone tinged slightly with blue; when struck it gives a clear ringing tone. Eventually innumerable formulae were evolved, but John Vickers was responsible for a great proportion of the marked ware until 1806. From 1806 to 1817 he continued the same mark but in larger letters. After 1837 his successors, Rutherford, Stacy, West & Company, reverted to the old mark but with BRITANNIA PLACE SHEFFIELD added below.

Other marks may be found, too. Kirby, Smith & Company made and marked Britannia metal from 1797; William Holdsworth from 1800; John Parker from 1821;

J. Wolstenholme from 1828; P. Ashberry from 1830; Broadhead & Atkins (eight crossed arrows) from about 1832. Birmingham's Matthew Boulton, who made Sheffield plate and silver, made Britannia metal from 1795 to 1809.

By 1817 Sheffield alone had seventy-three makers of the clean white ware. The trumpet and banner mark was used by James Dixon, one of the most notable makers, established in Sheffield in 1806 as Dixon & Smith; from 1833 his name James Dixon & Sons was followed by the words BEST BRITANNIA METAL. At the 1851 Exhibition he won a prize medal for tea and coffee services somewhat grudgingly praised as "imperfect imitations of silver, but the forms might be very advantageously imitated in that metal".

Only when collectors have a clear view of these developments can they discriminate between the rare early tin-and-temper pewter of the sad ware men and the tougher trifle, the less welcome heavily leaded or ley metal wares that continued the pewterers' traditional techniques and the subsequent emergence and early 19th-century dominance of the hard bluish metal with a soft polished brightness that was very nearly "fyne peauter" all over again under the name of Britannia metal.

Manufacturing techniques are a further guide. Whenever possible the old pewterer cast his vessels as single entities, finishing them in the lathe and by rasping and filing. The moulds were expensive equipment, often borrowed from the Guild, and the same mould might be used, for example, to shape the base of a late 17th-century candlestick and form a contemporaneous salt cellar. When necessary he cast his vessels in pieces and assembled by soldering—known as paling—and even in his solder the proportion of lead to tin increased, although as little solder as possible was used and the surface lathe-burnished with agate or bloodstone. Only over-aggressive cleaning is responsible for the untidy finish that may be seen today. In the days of the Company's power the interior surfaces of all domestic table ware had to be burnished too.

Ornament consisted of no more than light engraving in the soft surface—scratching to sarcastic silver engravers— and in dots and the short curves of self-explanatory wriggled or joggled engraving. Among early collectable pewter spoons the delightful cast finial was ornament enough—cone or acorn or maidenhead. Silver patterns set the style and indicate approximate dating. But this type of spoon with an added knop was lost before 1660 and after a spell with plain-cut ends fashion accepted the less individualistic patterns that could be achieved merely by flattening the stem end and giving it various small curves and notches.

The bowl itself is a guide to dating, being shallow at first and more or less fig-shaped, hardened by long hammering and strengthened at the back of the stem-bowl junction. Elliptical bowls were developed from about the mid-17th century and more egg-shaped bowls about a century later. The strengthening rib on the back of the bowl was extended into the familiar rat-tail later in the 17th century and low-relief ornament might appear on both sides of the stem, worked with steel dies lent out by the Pewterers' Company. The so-called Hanoverian spoons came with George I's court (1714), the end a plain arc with a thickened forward-pointing curve, so that the whole spoon was slightly S-shaped. The single arching curve from stem tip to bowl tip was introduced about the middle of the 18th century, presumably when spoons could be laid upon the table bowl upwards without becoming disfigured with dust or smuts. But these spoons were merely cast in gunmetal moulds, scraped and burnished with steel tools with little attempt to harden by hammering and the metal itself was ruined with lead. In Britannia metal spoons and ladles were made to the 1830s and here again silver styles help to date the thread and beaded edges, the shell to please the user's thumb, the waisted fiddle outline marking the silversmith's response to a taste for "revived rococo".

Many collectors delight in tankards and lidless mugs and these lingered on in homely tavern and chop house long after they were ousted by earthenwares for private use. Until the 18th century the tankard was vertically soldered into a tapering cylinder with soldered base raised on flared moulding and with a massive handle and a hinged lid opened by pressure upon an upstanding thumb-piece or purchase. Georgian tankards of the 1750s may be in the silversmiths' attractive tulip shape with beaded rim, high-domed lid and narrow moulded foot, and these were followed by ogee outlines in the 1760s and 1770s. More tulip outlines date to the early 19th century, however, with vertical rims. A satisfying shape in many Regency wares was the wide-bodied barrel with flat lid and plain D-curved handle.

In early Britannia metal the vessel was cut out in parts by die stamping and assembled by soldering. But after about 1820 this amenable metal could be shaped by spinning. This made the manufacture of hollow-ware a comparatively simple process. A disc of the metal was rolled to uniforn. thickness then placed against a shaped wooden block or chuck revolving in a lathe, being forced against it by a bright steel or hardwood tool until it took the required shape. The interior of a vessel may show traces of such spiralling pressure.

This spinning technique meant a considerable change in the look of such vessels as teapots. From the 1820s to about 1845 innumerable spun teapots delighted cottage families with their silver gleam. They had been made, of course, in the early versions of this hard pewter and there are records of them in the "French metal" of the 1770s, but those had been somewhat meagre little vessels, built up from soldered sections. When drop stamping made the shaping of these sections a speedy mechanical process it could include decoration in relief, but when the vessel was shaped by spinning its ornament had to be loaded upon the spout and feet. These were shaped by casting and relief ornament might be shaped in the same way and added as extraneous trimming throughout the era of "revived rococo" and the early Victorian delight in a profusion of naturalistic foliage such as vine and ivy.

Moulds for casting were ingeniously constructed in many parts, of brass, held together through the casting process by a covering of plaster of Paris easily broken for the vessel's removal. But these moulds were costly and when it became possible to cast a teapot complete with its spout, legs and relief ornament the mould might consist of as many as eighteen parts and cost perhaps £80.

Other vessels for the dresser include the two-handled loving cup, its double scroll handles and stemmed foot making it a shapely little piece dating to the later 18th and early 19th centuries. There are footed one-handled cups, too, and stemmed goblets. It is interesting to note that many stoneware vessels of the 19th century were fitted with Britannia metal lids when a heat-resistant stoneware was developed in the 1830s. These are often found with the crossed arrow mark of Broadhead & Atkins.

Pewter candlesticks have a long history, being cast, usually assembled by soldering and finished with lathe burnishing. Some of Charles II's day were hammered from sheet pewter in an attractive design with a cluster-column stem and a square drip flange above the square foot. The early 18th-century stick went through the delightful phases of its silver contemporary with a baluster stem on a domed foot, circular, hexagonal or octagonal and edged with light-dispersing gadroons. Eighteenth-century English brass was improved to make such delectable candlesticks that demand for pewter specimens declined, but in Britannia metal they may be found following the handsome neo-classic pillar notions of Sheffield plate.

Small pewter for the collector may include an early 18th century trencher salt with the same sparkling gadroons edging a capstan or spool outline. The flat trencher salt of the early 18th century may be found in round or octagonal outline; this was followed by the cup design, at first on a short stem and round foot and then on four tiny ball-and-claw feet. An inkstand, too, in capstan shape, turns up from time to time, made from the later 18th century onwards, and usually with the wide non-tip base plate that was essential in days of quill pens.

The rectangular box shape with centrally hinged covers is sometimes known as a treasury inkstand: these were made in several sizes through the 18th century. Others, even in everyday pewter, are in the tray shape with glass vessels for ink and pounce, just as mustard pots may be found with blue glass linings, and here a variant is the immovable lining of blue earthenware. An ingenious inkstand has been noticed with a square top and four holes for pens; below the ink are two small drawers, the lower one with a perforated base for sprinkling sand upon the wet writing.

In later pewter and Britannia metal the list of collectable items is almost endless, however. There are occasional miniature or toy pieces, as in brass and copper (Chapter Sixteen). These were made in some quantity from as early as the 17th century, but many more 200 years later. There are pipe tobacco stoppers and somewhat similar tiny seals but with monogram or device in reverse. There are pewter-mounted snuff mulls.

In the "fine pewter" of Britannia metal, today's collectables range from tea caddies to cruet frames, from fruit baskets to soup tureens, not to mention such one-time status symbols as wine coolers and trays for visiting cards. Pewter moulds with hinged sections produced highly ornamental jellies with such details as relief lattice patterns on the sides and other undercut detail that could not be turned out of the normal earthenware mould and gave the cook some satisfaction in puzzling her more observant guests.

Small flat-back ornaments such as dogs and horses were cast for the mantelshelf as silvery contrast to those of brass, but perhaps the most amusing mid-19th-century products, cast in poor-quality pewter or even in lead, were intended to be taken for medieval treasures. These are shaped as flattish pendants, sometimes seals or figurines, with odd little imagined-medieval figures shaped in relief, scraps of unintelligible lettering and arabic numerals. The ornament can be any kind of nonsense, but it can still rouse a tyro collector's interest today and soon enough these will be antiques in their own right as well as small symptoms of the escapist urge that produced them. Their makers were William Smith and Charles Eaton, who turned them out by the score from a workshop near the Tower and "found" them in the mud of the River Thames. To this day these primitive fakes are spoken of with affection rather than wrath or scorn as Billies and Charlies.

Chapter Eighteen

PATCHWORK COVERLETS AND QUILTS

O NE of the most delightful country cottages I know has a home-made patchwork quilt on every bed and a miniature version on a cot for the daughter's most favoured doll. Many of us go no further than dreaming about such luxury: the rest search high and low for the antique specimens and for scraps of contemporaneous materials that can make good any obvious signs of long wear since textiles, assuredly, however authentic, are ruined by shabbiness. Yet there is nothing fundamentally difficult about making a patchwork quilt. All that is needed is a collection of suitable sturdy scraps that associate well for the pleasure of their textures and the harmony of their colours— these and a timeless delight in plain, entirely self-effacing stitchery.

Much of the old patchwork found today is completely at home in the cottage for it represents the thrifty woman's inspired way of creating furnishings of lasting service as well as beauty from fragments of material too insignificant in themselves to be of any value. To many a cottager the scraps from some rich family must have met an intense hunger for colour and beauty so that the labour involved would have been joy indeed. At Anne of Cleves House, Lewes, a patchwork quilt worked by Flora Rosa Rumary (b. 1853) when she was a servant girl in her early teens was remembered by her later as giving her more pleasure than anything else in her life.

To purists, only the mosaic patchwork, the fabric composed entirely of the small patches, is acceptable but others include also the applied work wherein the patches merely contribute the pattern to a plain ground. The

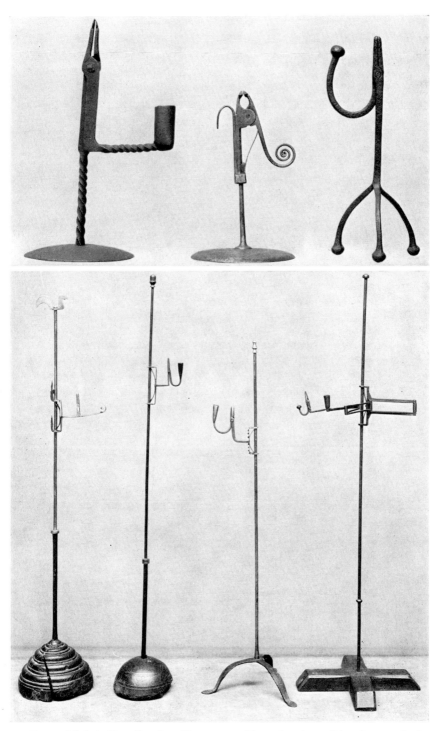

39. Iron rushlight holders. *Top:* for table use, two with cast iron bases. *Below:* floor standards, the tallest 4 feet 8 inches. These have adjustable spring clips. In one example the raised iron base serves instead of a safety stop low on the stem.

40. Pewter through three centuries. *Upper left:* spoons, 15th–16th century, with maidenhead and writhen knop finials. *Upper right:* Scottish wine measure or tappit hen, late 18th century, designed to thwart a wily potman trying to reduce its capacity. *Below:* pepper-pot and bowl cast and finished by turning and salt cellar with hammer-raised body marked with the crowned X of high quality ware.

Rumary quilt includes both techniques, the central square of plain fabric being purchased as a special luxury.

For the mosaic patchwork the medley of scraps of fabric were cut and stitched in the required shapes, most often geometrical, the shapes sewn together into smooth sheets of multicoloured pattern and these in turn often transformed into coverlets warm and enduring by means of the equally exacting and unostentatious stitchery involved in even the simplest quilting. Occasional comment from as early as medieval times suggests that chequered patchwork quilts have a far longer record than most people seem to assume.

Quilting, of course, was already an accepted necessity in medieval England, taken for granted and altogether too subdued for much mention among the records of glittering silk and gold. It made metal armour tolerable to the warring knight and gave the required air of leisured grandeur to the doublets and breeches of Tudor and Stuart fashion.

For women it meant the controlled shapeliness as well as the warmth of quilted coat and stomacher, of petticoat and pelisse in fashions that lasted far into Victorian days. But most especially one notes mention in old records of quilting as a strong, draught-excluding basis for bedchamber furnishing, for splendidly embroidered hangings, for coverings on showy daytime pillows to match the coverlets, for resilient under-mattresses and above all for covering the sleeper—"shining in gold and silver" as noted by Paul Hentzner on the huge state beds at Windsor in 1598, or "of yellow Indian stuff embroidered with birds and beasts and white silk fringe and tassels" as inventoried at Hardwick in 1601.

The craft of quilting appears in several forms. Basically the work consists of uniting two layers of woven fabric by lines of stitchery. Back stitch was customary for this work where a single ill-measured stitch could spoil a whole line of self-effacing neatness. From its term contrepointe it gave the coverlet its familiar name of counterpane. Usually but not invariably the quilter introduced an intervening layer of quilting cotton, wool or down evenly distributed by the stitchery. This not only contributed warmth and comfort but also emphasized stitching, the play of light and shadow depending upon the patterned spacing of the line-work. The experienced quilter took enormous trouble to achieve a flowing, well-balanced pattern, if necessary paying for professional help: a Mayfield schoolmaster in 1750 recorded his satisfaction in receiving half a guinea for five days work on such a drawing. Feathers, vines, baskets of flowers may be found as well as innumerable geometrical elaborations.

A third type of quilting popular in the 18th century, associated especially with bed coverlets, is now often known as Italian quilting. In this the pattern was empha-sized even more strongly by introducing soft cord or candlewick between the lines of stitching. The cord might be tacked in position on the lower sheet of fabric before stitching or poked or pulled into place afterwards.

To understand the association of quilting with patchwork it is necessary to realize the wide acceptance and importance of this quilted work that seems to have been appreciated as a craft for its decorative value only among the discriminat-ing few. One finds as a matter of course that the enterprising Mrs. Delany made quilts in the mid-18th century but even her admirers commented only on their flower embroidery. Today some collectors consider surface embroidery an unnecessary addition to the quilted pattern but accept the enrichment of embroidered eyelet holes introduced for ventilation and the muted shading of french knots like touches of stipple in a line engraving.

A damasked linen might form the upper surface of a quilt to rich effect. The lower side or backing was usually of cheaper stuff: even the Earl of Northampton (1614) had his popinjay green sarcenet lined with blue calico, which would less easily slide off the bed.

The public in general, however, merely bought plain quilting by the yard as a matter of course from "the poor quilters". *The London Tradesman* in 1747 declared that women and some men worked at the craft and "earn but little. They quilt likewise Quilts for Beds for the upholder . . . but nothing to get rich by . . ." Mrs. Purefoy as recorded in *The Purefoy Letters*, 1735–53, considered patterns and pieces "to make one of the new fashioned Low Beds without a Cornice" and bought forty-five yards at 10*s*. a yard. More came from abroad. The Portuguese colony of Goa long supplied elaborate coverlets, often with diapered grounds back-stitched in yellow silk. As early as 1614 the Earl of Northampton who revelled in rich fabrics owned "a China Quilt stitched in chequer work with yellow silk, the ground white".

Coverlets around the beginning of the 18th century were often of white silk quilted in yellow vermicular patterns of "Indian quilting" or in white linen or silk as a background to flower embroidery. This flat patterning of exotic flowers in chain stitch needle or tambour work was so widely accepted that in 1758 Johnson in the *Idler* referred to "three flourish'd quilts for every bed". An advertisement that I find interesting dating to 1730 shows that Joseph Patterson, a New Bond Street chair maker, supplied wool and cotton quilting as well as an assortment of other cheap goods such as painted floor cloths and, notably, basket-weave cradles. An occasional cradle in earthenware made as a gift "toy" records a forgotten custom by showing an outer covering in meander quilting to render it draughtproof.

The meander pattern may be regarded as the least creative and exacting form of quilting. Sometimes, I suspect, it was introduced merely to aid the imperfect embroiderer by minimizing such mishaps as puckering, much as the inexpert wood carver and silver worker in repoussé tended to cover their smooth, tell-tale background areas with all-over matting. What we lack as yet is any certainty as to when this unobtrusive background of quilting was combined with mosaic patchwork.

That patchwork too was accepted as commonplace in the early 18th century is indicated by casual references such as Swift's in *Gulliver's Travels*, 1726, to clothes that "looked like the patch-work made by the ladies in England, only that mine was all of a colour". It is possible to argue, however, that this refers to the type of patchwork known also as applied work. For today's collector the period of greatest interest begins late in the 18th century and is concerned more especially with the 19th, and it is interesting to note that the early 19th century which left us some of the finest patchwork coverlets produced comparatively little quilting.

Most patchwork of course is impossible to date. An occasional fragment of printed material may be dated to the 18th century but more to the 19th and there is no knowing how long it enjoyed a more fashionable existence before going to the patch bundle. From the late 1820s, for example, there was an air of better quality to the printed cottons but real knowledge of these fabric developments is specialist study. Here it is only possible to mention a few pointers. Floral prints on richly coloured grounds were in vogue around the turn of the century: by Victorian days there was a tendency for the lighter sprigs and spots of dress fabrics to be used instead of furnishing fabrics.

Early printing by wood blocks was supplemented, but not out-moded, by delicate line-work achieved with copper plates so that there is little guidance here but at least colour offers an occasional clue. A good substantial black is not to be found in 18th-century patterns, for example, and until at least 1809 any greens required were created by printing or hand pencilling a somewhat fleeting yellow over a printed blue. Sometimes a quilt in either mosaic or applied patch-work is found with an elaborate printed centrepiece. Thomas Sheraton mentioned these furnishings and they are now highly prized not only as splendid examples of elaborate calico printing but because they can be dated between about 1800 and 1817.

One of the most familiar celebrates George III's golden jubilee in 1809: a heavy grouping of flowers in a basket includes "G. 50. R" in the flower border. Another was made to mark the marriage of the ill-fated Princess Charlotte, its border announcing "Princess Charlotte of Wales married to Leopold Prince of Saxe Cobourg, May 2, 1816", an event that has left us a range of interesting souvenirs. Sometimes a printed snuff handkerchief found its way into a coverlet—source of innumerable subjects including amusing if some-what laboured comment upon current social life. But the authentic bed-cover print was made with border pieces to match. Apart from the interest of their dating these printed pieces are less attractive than the needlewoman's own notions.

41. Collectors' pieces in the sturdy successors to medieval pewter. *Top left:* teapot and stand in the straight lines that meant easy stamping and assembly and were equally popular with the factory silversmith. Here bright-cut ornament also copies silverwork. This is in Vickers white metal of the late 1780s and marked *I Vickers. Top right:* hot water jug in Britannia metal shaped by spinning. 1820s. *Centre:* Britannia metal dishes such as could be shaped by spinning but given an air of importance with cast handles and feet. *Bottom:* part of a tea service reflecting the 19th century's revival of attractive, surface-strengthening melon shaping.

42. Section of an 18th-century patchwork coverlet that measures 6 feet 3 inches by 4 feet 5½ inches. This is particularly interesting for the complicated arrangement of the tiny triangular patches that together form small squares with the pyramid effect popular in a range of home ornament from the late 18th century onwards. Some patches are of silk, some of velvet, but the decorative effect is mainly enhanced by the inclusion of regularly spaced squares containing embroideries in many contrasting styles.

Patchwork design depended upon a combination of tradition and individual inventiveness and some of the most interesting show obvious association with the older quilting tradition. The pieces may be cut in the quilter's geometrical shapes of diamonds, squares, triangles, the mid-19th century's most delightful hexagons and the challengingly difficult rounded triangles of the shell or scale pattern. Even when the pieces were cut out around a metal template and stiffened and edge-turned by tacking on to paper or card before being sewn together—the method of the practised worker—a pattern composed of curved edges proved extremely difficult. (The cards or papers—often old letters—were left in position until the work was completed and occasionally help to place a piece of unfinished work.)

Despite the problems, however, even an adaptation of the quilter's feather pattern is occasionally found: a mid-19th-century coverlet in the Victoria and Albert Museum is superbly worked with an intricate pattern dominated by curving outlines and shows the period's delight in rich fabrics and the contrasting matt and burnished surfaces of silk, satin and velvet.

The whole presentation of patchwork bore some relation to the early 19th century's general delight in mosaic pattern, expressed for example in cross stitch embroidery, bead work, even the geometrical devices of early Tunbridge ware, where a diversity of naturally grained and coloured wood veneers were fitted into orderly patterns. It is interesting to note too that in patchwork as in Tunbridge ware there was a mid-century tendency to reduce the size of the individual pieces so that occasionally a later 19th-century patchwork is composed of pieces less than an inch across. Pictorial patchworks too were made but have dated far more than formal patterns.

Often a patchwork of printed fabrics is combined with plain scraps surface embroidered, the contrasts in surface thus achieved requiring the formality of exact balance, such as the opposing triangular sections of each square or diamond in a design. The Victorians' so-called album quilts introduced signatures and dates embroidered on some of the patches. But the real find is the signature of the maker in some inconspicuous corner. A child's work was often marked with the name and age so that all could marvel at such precocity—and that at least is something we have not ceased to wonder at today.

Most attractive perhaps are the patchwork patterns where simple geometrical shapes are exactly interworked by the lines of quilting. For example a simple patchwork of squares may be transformed by squares of quilting, their corner mitres meeting exactly in the centres of the patches. Craft publications of the 19th century name a range of patterns that the collector can identify.

Any visitor to the magnificent American Museum near Bath must be impressed by the spectacular collection of American patchwork but the Englishwoman too had her windmill, star, pincushion, jewel, lozenge, pavement, log cabin, Chinese box—to which traditional quilting patterns could be applied and which in turn reflected current fashions such as the hob nail and strawberry diamonds of the Regency glass-cutter as well as such timeless patterns as the hearts of the marriage quilt. More scope for imaginative colour schemes was available to the woman who was not too thrifty to buy the pound bundles of scraps available from silk mercers and linen drapers in the second half of the century, such as suitably tinted muslins.

Among applied patchwork a wider range of pattern was possible and the work was less exacting as the pieces had merely to be sewn to a firm ground such as calico. The first half of the 19th century produced some delightful flower and basket compositions with the imaginative application of flowered scraps but later the tendency was towards clear-cut geometrical designs. One advantage was the opportunity to introduce scraps unsuitable for more wear-exacting mosaic work.

By then the early 19th-century fashion for edging a coverlet with a fringe of linen was somewhat outmoded. Silk patches had to be edged with fringes of heavy yellow silk. Between the patches, too, outlines of pattern might be emphasized by braid or silk stitchery. From about 1850 a favourite was a running stitch such as coral or herringbone worked in the softly glossy silk known as filoselle, obtained from the least valuable part of the silkworm cocoon.

Crazy quilts were perhaps the least attractive Victorian notion for patchwork, with a medley of overlapping irregularly shaped scraps entirely covering a linen or cotton base, their outlines masked by running stitches and the patches themselves erratically embroidered and loaded with additional ornament such as ribbons and beads.

For the cottage, quilting and patchwork are at their most delightful as bed furnishings but the collector must remember that when patchwork was welcomed in the Victorian drawing room all manner of small articles were created including cushions, hand screens, pincushions, in velvets and silks sometimes at least with an eye for colour harmony and a brilliance of technique that would put most of us to shame today.

Chapter Nineteen

PRINTS more than most antiques and curios suffer from a surfeit of technical terms. The would-be collector is so hedged around with warnings about faked "states", missing "plate marks", superimposed margins, worn plate surfaces and inked-in detail that the print as a pleasure to look upon never emerges at all. This is nonsense for the whole purpose of any print is to be looked at and enjoyed. Some may be regarded as art forms in their own right, created by artists and only a little less individualistic than these artists' paintings or drawings: in this class of rare treasure come the most famous Rembrandt etchings or Paul Sandby aquatints. But for most of us as for the public of their day prints are go-betweens, linking famous artists with those who could never hope to see, let alone to buy, many of their originals.

This now may seem a minor service but through the 18th and early 19th centuries that produced the prints we collect today the artist himself was a vital link in the social structure. Celebrities, beauties, important events, famous or notorious scenes depended largely upon the artist for their recognition. And if artists were the court photographers and social historians the prints taken in quantity from their unique originals had to serve alike as the society glossies and pictorial dailies, recording inevitably much that has lost its savour but also much that is still poignant, still vivid with the life of yesterday—infinitely worth preserving in folios for occasional review or as constant, companionable wall decoration.

The men who created these prints were often astonishingly expert craftsmen and like all purpose-serving good

184

craftsmanship their technique is a lasting delight. But the inexpert cottage collector today is best advised to collect first and foremost for the subject matter and treatment that appeals with no thought for clever investment. This surely was the way the prints were sought and bought by their original collectors who could thus associate themselves with the lively world around them, laughing at Cruikshank's winners of the Dunmow Flitch, decrying a too pompous politician, living for a moment more richly and excitingly than their own narrow circumstances were ever likely to allow.

It is not difficult to understand the continuing demand for the genuine Alken etching with its intensity of delight in man's association with horses, or for the old bird or flower engraving that conveyed not only the facts but a little of man's capacity to marvel. No written advice can safeguard beginners from collecting prints that the more expert would reject for a score of reasons but it may help them to understand what they are seeing and look again with greater confidence and pleasure.

There are many ways for the maker of prints to reproduce the artist's line-work: the real problem always has been to convey the effect of his subtler achievements in colour and texture. As the purpose was always to take a considerable number of prints from a single copying of the artist's picture the medium had to be hard and basically hostile to the subtleties of brush stroke. Until the remarkable discovery of lithography this meant a basis of wood or metal. Wood was of early but limited use; far greater ingenuity is found in the preparations for printing from metal and these are what collectors are most likely to find confusing, or deeply absorbing.

Woodcuts tend to be skimpy little crudities, torn from old books or broadsides, but the first time a collector encounters, unglazed, a fine-quality mezzotint he realizes why so many men, considerable artists in their own right, were prepared to submit to the long, exhausting disciplines of the print-maker. The woodcut is simple as a fingerprint. With most of the surface cut away the design was left as thin lines in higher relief that, when dipped in ink, would make corresponding marks in reverse upon the paper: this is known as a relief process. The plank or side grain of soft, lightly-grained pear or lime wood was used but with little subtlety in the result.

Wood engraving is a more confusing term and is usually applied to the style of woodcut associated with Thomas Bewick in the last quarter of the 18th century, over a century after the craft of the woodcut had lost favour to metal engraving. In the wood engraving the end grain of boxwood was used. It was still a relief process, the heavy ink being impressed upon the paper from the projecting parts of the surface. But Bewick altered the whole effect, working out his theme largely with the delicate cutting strokes of the engraver on metal, then the customary practice. On the wood block such cuts removed the surface and therefore conveyed the picture by lines of white upon the print. Albrecht Dürer showed what could be achieved with woodcuts. In the 19th century wood engraving was continued by Luke Clennell, J. W. Whymper and others, such as the familiar book illustrations by the Dalziel brothers after designs by J. E. Millais and other popular artists.

In contrast the metal engraver worked by what is known as an intaglio process, a term applied to all the methods of printing that depend upon hollows in the metal to retain the ink when the top surface is wiped clean, or nearly clean, and to convey it under pressure to the paper. The ink can be felt with the finger tips as a slight texture on the paper surface: the engraved die and resultant personal notepaper heading is an obvious example. Intaglio prints include etchings, line and stipple engravings, drypoints and aquatints. Lithography, without either ridges or hollows, working on the resist principle common to several important crafts of its day, comes under the heading of surface print. It is so comparatively simple that had it been discovered earlier we might never have inherited the far more exciting styles of print men wrested from their intaglio processes on metal.

These show various methods of working upon the metal to convey in ink the artist's information, their deviousness due to the wish to give a sympathetic rendering of flesh and fabric, cloud and landscape. The most obvious was to cut away fragments of the metal with a fine graving tool or burin. The 18th century's fine copper plate enabled the engraver to produce extremely delicate line-work, pushing the burin or graver with its handle in the hollow of his palm and removing the tiny curls or burrs of cut metal with a scraper. The copper plate had to be pressed extremely hard upon the paper and it was seldom possible to take more than about 200 impressions without touching up the plate. No printing from woodcut or from the lithographer's stone ever achieved the clear, strong, endlessly varied lines of such engraving.

Prints have been made from line engravings from the 15th century and the craft was already old then to the goldsmith but in the 18th century it was especially a French enthusiasm. William Hogarth (1697–1764) made both line engravings and etchings. Robert Strange and William Sharp may be mentioned and the landscapes of William Woollett. Inevitably the process was used for endless copying of the work of every popular artist and the collector has to pick warily. Even the atmospheric effects of Turner were presented by such men as W. B. Cooke, E. Goodall, J. T. Willmore and J. Pye.

A variant of line engraving is known as drypoint. Collectors may find references to its use by the etcher, including Rembrandt, but that is merely a confusion. The basic process was to scrape hollow lines in the metal, the tool being a pencil-like point of steel, the movement a drawing stroke rather than the strong but controlled pushing motion used with a graver. Thus the burr of displaced metal rose always beside the hollowed line and in this work it was not scraped away. The ink it absorbed gave the printed line a velvety edge although it was soon flattened, sometimes after as few as fifty impressions had been taken.

Collectors look for 18th-century work by Thomas Worlidge and Benjamin Wilson and in the early 19th century by David Wilkie and Andrew Geddes. After about 1820 steel might be used instead of copper for a line engraving or a mezzotint though necessarily a softer steel than the engraver's tools. Once electro-plating was established in the 1840s a thin coating of steel could be applied to the copper with equally enduring service, which was mainly required for such large printings as book illustrations.

The logical development from the drypoint was the process that in effect created a surface of burrs all over the metal plate so that if inked it would print entirely in a velvety black. From such a basis the artist-craftsman could proceed to flatten and reduce the burr effect to achieve his lighter tones, culminating in highlights where the metal was rendered entirely smooth with a burnisher. This to many is the most exciting style of print since it abandoned the attempt to express the artist's brush work in lines or dots or close networks of shading and concentrated instead on tone effects, still with no intermediary between tool and metal.

The notion of the mezzotint engraving originated with Ludwig von Siegen (1609–76) but is associated especially with Prince Rupert (1619–82). By the end of the 17th century the method had become known as *la manière anglaise*. Many English names may be mentioned among 18th century and Regency engravers in mezzotint including James McArdell, Richard Houston, John Dixon, Valentine Green, John Raphael Smith, William Pether. Portraits especially were reproduced with great subtlety: Reynolds, Gainsborough and Romney were copied by more than a hundred mezzotint engravers and Turner, Constable and Morland were widely popularized by Charles Turner, T. G. Lupton, David Lucas, William Ward and many others. J. C. Le Blon (1667–1741) was the first to experiment with three-colour mezzotints.

It is easy to give too much attention to mezzotint engravings which could be printed only in small numbers and were essentially for the folios of the rich. But it was important at the time: for example, a beauty painted by Gainsborough or Reynolds could have her portrait copied in this way and much of its original quality conveyed to her friends and admirers. Many ordinary little prints of famous beauties came from workaday engravers copying the mezzotints rather than the original paintings.

43a. Simple background quilting in the popular early 18th-century manner when a coverlet was often composed of two layers of material: this was sturdy, draped well on the bed and presented an attractive surface texture. Such meticulous backstitching may be found under flower embroidery worked in solid colour finely graded and shaded by the use of close chain-stitch.

43b. Small section from a coverlet showing diamond quilting as the background linking a fascinating collection of different motifs worked in silks on linen in the early 18th century when Englishwomen were enthralled by Oriental design but could interpret it with humour too.

44a. To Henry Alken, hard-riding horseman, in such a print only the animal mattered, presenting a superb study in movement and texture. The print is captioned "By the Lord Harry my Chestnut Horse can almost fly" and marked *H. Alken del et sculp* indicating that he engraved the scene from his own original composition. This dates to 1829.

44b. Mezzotint by William Ward, A.R.A., after George Morland's original "The Turnpike Gate", showing the sense of atmosphere achieved only with this, the most rewarding process known to the print-maker.

The method involved laboriously preparing the metal plate by roughening it all over with a rocker, a tool with a curved serrated edge of close-set cutting teeth. The tool was worked across the metal in numerous criss-cross lines until the surface was covered with tiny hollows and their accompanying burrs. The craftsman worked on this with a mezzotint scraper, removing the burrs to the required extent for tone contrast while retaining a rich shadowy effect.

To many collectors, however, a print implies a use of acid rather than tools to bite into the metal, as in etching, stipple and aquatint. These gave the craftsman a kindlier surface for creating his picture which could more closely resemble freehand drawing. Indeed the etching is essentially the original work of an artist rather than the translated work "after" some famous artist most usually found in line engraving and aquatint.

The metal was covered with a thin layer composed of waxes, gums or resins. This was more or less transparent but could be blackened with a lighted taper so that the artist could see the lines drawn into it with an etching needle. These required little effort or special technique to cut through to the copper and when the plate was immersed in aqua fortis this ate into this exposed metal to the depth required. Usually this was a repetitive process, the plate being removed from the acid and some lines protected by varnish, then returned to the acid for further emphasis to be given to other detail as often as might be required. From time to time the artist checked his progress by taking a proof print from the metal and when necessary could apply charcoal to modify lines etched too deeply. The deeper the acid bit into the plate the more ink these lines would retain to produce greater strength of tone in the print.

With acid there was of course no burr and the artist did not need the engraver's manual skill. For a softer line he might work with a pencil over thin paper spread upon a softer wax composition. A little of the wax came away with the paper and the lines cut with the etching acid were considerably softer. Henry Alken, for example, sometimes used this soft-edged etching which may suggest a pencil drawing but the process was ousted by lithography.

Even when the etcher kept to the somewhat formal exactitude of the line engraver it is usually possible to distinguish which method has been used as the etcher's lines cut by the acid lack the delicate tapering points typical of the line engraving. Rembrandt is considered the greatest of all etchers but famous artists have delighted in the freedom of this work, including many of the 19th century from William Blake and Edwin Landseer to J. M. W. Turner and J. McNeill Whistler. The clear but casual line-work suited caricature and satire. Etchings by Thomas Rowlandson, James Gillray, George Cruikshank are endlessly sought after but there were many others who might be mentioned such as Charles Keene, Samuel Palmer, Andrew Geddes, David Wilkie.

Stipple was a variant of etching that collectors love or hate on sight. Here as in some later Impressionist painting gradations of tone were attempted by means of innumerable tiny dots or in the short strokes known as flicks. The basic outlines and shadow were introduced with an etching needle or a roulette tool through the waxy ground and cut with acid as in etching, but the print was given its character by the work done directly upon the plate with a curving-pointed stipple-engraver. Some workers in stipple adapted the silversmith's punch tools, either hand pressed or hammered. All that mattered was the placing and "texture" of the dots.

From the pure stipple developed the so-called crayon engraving produced by stippling the surface with roulettes that would create a grain effect suggesting chalk lines. Pure stipple and this less laboured effect were often combined. The method is often considered to produce effeminate prints and it is not surprising to find them more often in gentle tones of brown or red than in black. Coloured stipple engravings were sometimes made by dabbing the plate with different colours where required between each printing. The result somewhat suggests coloured pastel work, often in blue and red of various tints reinforced with black. If the colour is not entirely confined to the dots or flicks the print has been hand coloured after printing.

Stipple was essentially delicate work and suited the mood

of the late 18th century. It was introduced to this country by W. W. Ryland (1738–93). Francesco Bartolozzi (1728–1813) settled in London in 1764 and promptly became engraver to George III. He produced stipple-engraved portraits of beauties of the day after Reynolds, Gainsborough, Romney and Downham. The somewhat effeminate style of such artists as Angelica Kaufmann, Richard Cosway and Francis Wheatley was reproduced in stipple engravings of varying quality: names to look for in the 18th and early 19th centuries include Thomas Burke, Thomas Cheesman, Charles Wilkin, J. P. Simon.

The other acid etching process is aquatint, introduced no earlier than the 1760s and used especially to reproduce the effects of wash drawings. The Spanish artist Goya used the process frequently and in England it was put to fine effect by Paul Sandby in several of his series of views from 1775. The works of Rowlandson, Alken and other early 19th-century artists were widely reproduced in aquatint but not many were made after about 1840. English names to look for include Thomas Malton in the later 18th century, Thomas and William Daniell continuing through the 1830s, R. and D. Havell and Richard Golding.

This process, too, involved the use of acid to do the work of creating hollows in the metal plate but here the effect required was a picture expressed in washes of different tones and the aqua fortis was applied in areas rather than lines or dots. To be conveyed by the technique of printing this meant creating a surface texture: this was achieved by filtering the acid through a porous ground. This effect could be produced by several methods—even to some extent by applying sandpaper to a line engraving—but most usually the ground was of resin, either applied as a powder or dissolved in spirits of wine which evaporated to leave a suitable fine-grained surface covering. Here again depth of tone depended upon the cumulative effect of repeated immersions in the acid, each detail on the plate being protected from further onslaughts as soon as it was considered that it would print with enough intensity of tone. Thus only the white areas of the print entirely escape the pleasing granular effect, the artist working from light to dark.

191

Aquatints too were printed in colour using a number of plates each prepared so as to contribute part of the print. But by 1840 new ideas were revolutionizing colour printing and among these every beginner-collector has heard of Baxter prints. Le Blon (1670-1741), as I mention above, first thought out how to produce mezzotints in the full range of rainbow colours. He used a plate for each of the primary colours, red, yellow, blue and by superimposing these colours sought to achieve varying tones of secondary and tertiary colours too—blue on yellow to make green and so on. Every school child with a paint-box knows the theory and how inadequate the results tend to be.

George Baxter's prints were made under a patent of 1836 extended to 1855. Again the principle was a series of plates meticulously superimposed, each conveying a different colour or tone, sometimes as many as eighty. His particular pride was that they should suggest oil paintings and his prints draw attention to this use of oil colours, but even this elaborate and extraordinarily successful work required a basis in the print maker's technique of dark lines and stipple. Thus the framework to this colour was a key-plate with the whole scene worked out upon it using the aquatint method of engraving for a general basis, etching for delicate lines and stipple for flesh work.

Collectors find innumerable mediocre prints applied to humble purposes but Baxter also issued 400 of high quality and these are still collectors' magic. The first, "The Departure of Camden", came in 1838 but the most spectacular was his "Coronation of Queen Victoria", with some 200 recognizable portraits. His flower prints are delightful, but some such as "Hollyhocks" and "The Gardener's Shed" have been reproduced widely. From 1849 he licensed the process to A. le Blond—not to be confused with the earlier Le Blon—and to J. Mansell, J. M. Kronheim and others whose names are familiar to collectors of Victorian valentines, Christmas cards and other delightful *billets-doux*.

Collectors must note that Le Blond acquired sixty-nine sets of Baxter plates and colour blocks in 1868: prints from these are inferior and known as Le Blond-Baxters. Early Baxter work shows the imprint on the print itself; from 1848

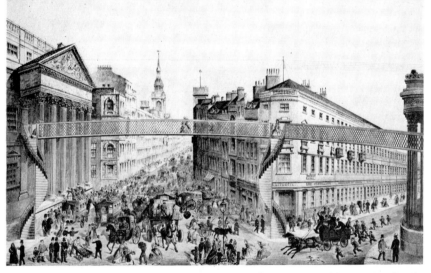

45. Contrasting processes for producing prints. The well-known Reynolds portraits of Lady Smith and her family (*upper left*) are reproduced in the slightly effeminate effect of stipple by Francesco Bartolozzi, R.A., with great delicacy of tone and texture. *Upper right:* a vivid Baxter print, "The Morning Call". The brass plate on the door bears Baxter's name and on the lower step the snow is inscribed: PUBLISHED SEPT 1ST 1853 BY G. BAXTER PROPRIETOR AND PATENTEE LONDON. *Below:* hand-coloured lithograph of a proposed street bridge at Mansion House, London, 1840. This anonymous scene indicates the detail that can be achieved despite the comparatively soft outlines of this medium.

46a. Delightful study of two ruffs and a reeve from R. I. Selby's *Illustrations of British Ornithology*. This work is dated 1834, showing late and technically expert use of copper-plate engraving coloured by hand.

46b. "Dr. Syntax landing at Calais", from the three *Tours of Dr. Syntax*, humorous verses by William Combes issued 1815–21 and familiar today for their Thomas Rowlandson illustrations. Here, by the aquatint process, an effect is achieved somewhat resembling a wash drawing in water colour.

it appeared on the mount and the red oval containing his name and address and the subject title appeared in 1849. This "Baxter seal" was changed to white in 1850.

Lithography comes last in this survey because it was a very different notion, invented in the 1790s and the delight of every artist with an eye for publicity until it degenerated into a commercial tool in the 1850s. The basis was a fine-textured stone, though some metals such as aluminium proved equally effective. This the artist drew upon as freely as upon paper, using a form of greasy chalk. The grease left upon the stone repelled water so that when the stone was saturated only the artist's work was unaffected and therefore still able to absorb the ink passed over it on a roller.

The printed result might suggest a chalk drawing and the clear lines of metal engraving were never entirely recaptured: a comparison, say, of an Audubon aquatint with the commoner lithographed copy showing the loss of vigour. but many varieties were possible. The stone might be largely covered with the greasy chalk (which then of course when inked would print black) and this might be worked upon with a point to result in a printing of fine white lines. Or finer lines might be worked upon the stone by using a solution of the lithographic chalk applied with a pen. Even a drawing on paper could be transferred to the stone.

Here the field of the collector is immense. There are superb views by R. P. Bonington, for example, and clear delicate work by Richard Lane. James Ward is associated with animal subjects. John Gould made many delightful drawings of birds, lithographed by his wife and others, though here it would be hard to rival Edward Lear's lively parrots. Flower studies may be found by Valentine Bartholomew, for example, and landscapes by George Barnard, J. C. Bourne and many others. Joseph Nash did original work as well as reproducing David Wilkie and others; John Doyle is noted for his political commentaries.

The beginner collector can get by with only a few technical terms. State and proof are words variously interpreted and it is enough for the beginner to realize that prints—"impressions"—may be taken from a plate or stone at many stages to see how the work is progressing and again when it is finished before the different lines of lettering are added underneath.

These tiny pieces of information at the bottom are important however. "Original engraving", for example, is just a print like any other but one that was designed as well as cut by the engraver. An engraving "after" an artist is a copy and may be a very long way from the original painting. Of the latin words, *sculpsit* (*sculp.*, *sc.*) and also *caelavit* and *incidit* indicate the engraver; *fecit* (literally 'he made') most usually means the etcher; *excudit* (*excud.*, *ex.*) and *formis* indicate the publisher or print seller; *divulgavit* means 'published'; *lith.* or *lith. by* usually indicates the lithographic printer but sometimes the man who drew the picture upon the stone; *delineavit* (*del.*) more specifically the draughtsman or the artist who drew the original which the engraver copied; *figuravit* means 'drew'; *pinxit* (*pinx.*) 'painted'; *invenit* means 'designed'. Thus when a genuine Alken print is lettered H. *Alken del. et sculp.* it means that he was his own designer of the original drawing that he himself engraved upon the metal—and how infinitely superior to those who copied him! One other detail. A print often gives a date together with the words "Published according to Act of Parliament". Acts dealing with copyright were passed from 1735 onwards but the date must be taken as that of the most recent previous act and not of the print itself.

Chapter Twenty

ENGLISH MAPS

FEW of us, I suppose, can regard maps dispassionately. Either they appear deliberately hostile in their incomprehensibility or they welcome us like a hilltop panorama. To the collector old maps offer journeys in time as well as place, their details of fact and fancy begin at the very heart of fairy tale. The earliest detailed map of Britain now in existence was made about 1250 by Matthew Paris of St. Albans. This was prepared not so much as a presentation of geographical fact but to serve as a travellers' touring chart showing pilgrims the towns and religious houses where they could stay on their way to Dover en route for Rome, and maps with a special individualistic purpose have been among the most intriguing ever since. This particular specimen is a strange distortion but Paris was more forward-looking than some of his successors in his introduction of conventional signs—the map-addict's special joy—and marginal notes.

Subsequent centuries saw the map-makers of different European countries leading the world in this skilled craft. The Italians were pre-eminent through much of the 16th century, the Flemish and Dutch from late in that century until the end of the 17th and thereafter the French, before English map-makers came into their own from about the end of the 18th century.

Through the collectors' period it is possible to trace these foreign influences in our own countrymen's maps of the British Isles but it would be strange indeed if there were no pitfalls for collectors who rely on dates and signatures. Everything about an old map can contribute to its story— the way it is printed, the treatment of each formalized detail, the style of its lettering, the cartouche or other ornament around its title, the colouring or lack of it, even the paper itself. Only if all these tally with its purported date can the collector begin to feel pleased that his find is authentic and not merely some later reprint or modern imitation.

A few Englishmen contributed notably to our records of this country. There was George Lily, for example, who brought to England in 1555 the first "modern" map of the British Isles, its exquisitely delicate details engraved and printed in Rome not long before printing from engraved copper plates was introduced to England by Flemish craftsmen to the detriment of the more heavy-handed wood-cut and rarer wood engraving. (The other method of printing maps, by lithography, was a 19th-century development.) Christopher Saxton (*c.* 1542–1610) issued his now rare *Atlas of the Counties of England* in 1579 containing thirty-five double-page folio maps and a plate showing the "Arms of the Peers", all comprehensively indexed. He spent nine years surveying and mapping the counties of England and Wales with considerable accuracy, the more remarkable when it is remembered that these were the first county maps ever printed. Some of the maps pre-date the issue of the whole atlas. Some are coloured but the un-coloured are now the more sought after. Especially prized are those including the name of one of Saxton's engravers, Augustine Ryther.

As early as 1607 and as late as 1749 Saxton maps were reprinted. It is interesting to note that his excessively rare *Britannia Insularum*, scaled at 8 miles to the inch, was re-issued in 1687 by Philip Lea. Typically, Lea used the old copper plates but altered many details, adding roads, for example, copied from another map-maker Ogilby, and even altering the ships from Elizabethan to Stuart rig. But this, too, is now rare. Collectors are right to stress the supreme importance of Saxton but must recognize that his popularity shows with unwelcome frequency in maps directly derived from him, issued until as late as 1799.

Neither Saxton nor John Speed marked roads on their maps. Probably they knew from their surveying journeys how unpredictable these could be. The first county maps marking major roads—rarities, too—were produced by John Norden (1548–1625), whose Middlesex appeared in 1593. It was Norden in his *Guyde to English Travellers*, 1625, who thought first of triangular distance tables that tell at a glance the distance between any two towns. But the most intriguing route maps of the 17th century were by John Ogilby. These were drawn as vertical strips, about seven to a sheet, taking the traveller from town to town in the AA manner of today. His *Britannia* dates to 1675. A typical sheet would take a traveller, strip by strip, from London through Acton, Uxbridge, Aylesbury to Buckingham and thence over the Oxfordshire border to Banbury. He listed distance between the towns measured with a waywiser. By then the chain of 22 yards had been introduced—in 1624—but most map-makers still used varying lengths of mile or league: he was the first to use the statute mile of 1,760 yards.

After Norden and Ogilby all maps had to show roads, including later editions of Saxton and others. John Senex, for instance, in 1719 issued a hundred maps of the principal roads in England and Wales on the Ogilby model. With such a subject it is impossible not to digress and to mention here the small county atlases made by John Cary in the late 18th century which used this strip technique to delight the many travellers to spas and resorts. Cary drew lines from his roads showing where the traveller could view imposing residences near his route and was human enough to include the names of the owners.

John Speed (1552–1629) was a notable early maker of county maps, copying, with acknowledgments, from Saxton and others where necessary but expressing in his maps his own particular delight in decorative and historical detail. His huge *Theatre of the Empire of Great Britaine* contains fifty-four maps measuring 20 inches by 15, so big that he had them printed in Holland. Sometimes an early single sheet is found dating a year or two before publication in 1611 but all too often ruined by modern colouring. To take but one example, in Cornwall he credits his facts to Norden but includes not only a setting of ships and creatures in the "British See" but eight Cornish coats of arms and a detailed picture of Launceston. He issued, too, a pocket atlas and this also has appeared again and again. His, it may be mentioned, was the first Englishman's *Prospects of the Most Famous Parts of the World* another work with a long history.

Speed in his turn was copied to a large extent in the *Atlas of England and Wales*—part iv of the beautifully presented *Theatrum Orbis Terrarum* by G. & J. Blaeu who contributed notably to the mapping of Scotland.

County maps tend to be especially endearing, particularly if it is possible to assemble several of a favourite county drawn at different periods and frequently proving increasingly interesting as they approach modern times. Probably the strangest in any such collection would be from Michael Drayton's *Polyolbion* issued in parts in 1612 and 1622. Here an occasional town name and many rivers form the background to a scattering of attractive little figures at country tasks and more surprising ladies wearing the conventional town sign as headgear. He even included beckoning water nymphs in the rivers. It is not always realized, of course, that many makers of large-scale maps introduced small figures, such as wagoners, harvesters and the like with a purpose. They took their cue from the hand-drawn estate maps—themselves fascinating but rare acquisitions—where the use of each field and track had to be indicated. Sea monsters we must assume merely met the need to fill unacceptable bare spaces.

John Seller (1647–1701) was another innovator. In 1676 he took London—St. Paul's—as the prime meridian on his maps: so it remained on most English maps for more than a century before changing to Greenwich in 1794. His title of Hydrographer to Charles II and succeeding monarchs indicates his main concern for nautical charts and the like, and he produced the first pocket atlas of the stars. Nevertheless Samuel Pepys complained that Seller "had bought the old worn Dutch copper plates for old copper and had refreshed them in many places".

A glimpse of the massive baroque style of Dutch mapmaking was offered to London by Herman Moll who settled there in 1688, remaining till his death in 1732 and producing maps of many parts of the world illustrated with figures in their national costumes. In his *New Description of England and Wales*, 1724, his page margins are filled with his curious little figures; his Scotland carries views of the principal towns.

Those of us with an affection for maps can never have the scale large enough, the factual detail sufficiently elaborated. *The Cities of London, Westminster and Southwark* on a scale of 5 inches to the mile from the Huguenot refugee John Rocque, 1746, are welcome indeed. Rocque made large-scale county maps, too, derived inevitably from the now excessively rare *Britannia Insularum* of Saxton but introducing his own treatment of hill and farm, orchard and woodland evolved during early work on estate plans. Rocque was responsible also for an atlas entitled *London and the Country near Ten Miles Round*.

A little later, around 1770, Thomas Jefferys issued a number of good county maps, including some on a scale of 2 inches to the mile. But perhaps the maps of this period that most nearly absorb us into their realm are the counties engraved by George Bickham junior for *The British Monarchy or a New Chorographical Description of all the Dominions Subject to the King of Great Britain*, published 1749. Indeed these can scarcely be called maps. In each of forty-eight engravings Bickham presents a bird's-eye view of a whole county, its hills and woodlands, towns, villages, boats, figures, wagons and all, with town names here and there which he must surely have felt were intrusive.

Among late map-makers for the collector John Cary (1754–1835) has been mentioned already. He is especially notable for superbly engraved, wholly functional and unornamented maps late in the 18th century. More in character with their times were some of the early 19th-century map-makers who reflected current delight in picturesque views by including appealing little vignettes. This of course was a notion going right back to the days of John Norden. Old St. Paul's and an immensely lively Nonsuch Palace are important among Speed's contributions, but the records of this country in the early 19th century were unsurpassed, despite the fact that map-makers were beginning their losing fight against the factual efficiency of the Ordnance Survey whose Kent appeated in 1801.

Langley's *New County Atlas*, 1817–18, was especially attractive: Kent, for example, shows hop-pickers at work and a ploughing team against a background of Chatham dockyard. T. Moule (1784–1851) in *The English Counties Delineated*, 1836–39, shows delicate draughtsmanship in the up-and-coming craft of lithography. His Sussex, for example, shows Brighton Chain Pier, Chichester Cathedral and Arundel Castle; Gloucestershire, the Cathedral, Tewkesbury Abbey church and the New Spa, Cheltenham, with tiny figures on tree-shaded lawns and also a glimpse of maidens drinking from a more romantic fountain.

Sometimes the map lacks a maker's or engraver's name or the name is suspect. Often and often a costly copper-plate engraving of a map had its date changed, new facts added until its original creator may be hard to recognize. Pepys knew that, as early as the 17th century. Worst of all are maps copied, date and all, by more recent engravers. Often when lacking a name the collector can find other clues to a map's age and can soon detect the anachronism that betrays the inexpert imitator. The cartouche presenting the map's title is a personal affair, treated casually or importantly as the engraver thought fit, but treated nevertheless in a style acceptable to its period. The early framing was the Italian's Renaissance strapwork, basically composed of formal "three-dimensional" scrolls but enlivened with all manner of queer little details from signs of the zodiac to groups of fruit. Ornament soon spilled over into the maps' borders where Speed introduced the fashion for showing town plans and gaily costumed celebrity figures. (Norden, on the other hand, merely squared his maps and used the borders for numbers along the top and letters down one side to simplify cross-references in the modern atlas manner.)

In the 17th century the Flemish and Dutch map-engravers developed the baroque style with magnificent, overpowering cartouches heavy with scrolls and tasselled draperies and often peopled with groups of figures in colourful costumes. Boys or amorini frolicked in many unlikely places in late Stuart days here as well as on the Continent: Saxton, for example, had introduced them as early as the 1570s, the Blaeus with their Dutch background delighted in them in the 1640s, Ogilby in 1675. But they were in their element among the compasses, measuring wheels and other surveyor's instruments and continued in the lighter rococo style of cartouche made fashionable by the French through their near-century of pre-eminence from about 1700. There is a world of difference between the buxom figures of Plenty and Wisdom heavily supporting a formal crested shield of the later 17th century and the scatter of cupids around a wildly asymmetrical cartouche composed of opposing C-scrolls and as likely as not set in a scene of pastoral ruins such as dominated mid-18th-century ideas.

The pastoral scenes and romantic ruins that were the accepted basis of so much casual ornament in the later 18th century found their way on to many a map title. And from late Stuart days onwards, it seems, until the 19th century there was uncomplaining acceptance, too, of the Four Continents, the Elements and similarly easily identifiable ladies equally familiar on post-Restoration embroidery, enamelled snuffbox of the 1760s and painted clock face of the century's end.

Some cartographers made even their cartouches of asymmetrical scrolls wholly personal and delightful: for example, Emanuel Bowen's West Riding of Yorkshire from his *Large English Atlas*, 1749-55, offers a formal scroll-framed dedication to the Marquis of Rockingham but around the title he shows the story of the woollen trade— sheep being shorn, a traveller buying wool, a woman at her spinning wheel, weaving equipment and bales of cloth with pine trees and waterfalls to give the authentic setting and, for good measure, an open knife box in the foreground to acknowledge the Sheffield cutlers—and even at that I have left some details unelucidated. Peat-cutting with its special tools and techniques illustrates his map of Huntingdonshire.

Inevitably the 19th century with its admiration for romantic Elizabethan notions tended to return to the early style of formal strapwork, Gothic title lettering and the like. The lettering, of course, is another important factor. The very early black letter of Matthew Paris gave way generally in the later 15th century to the cursive script evolved in Rome. Thereafter most map-engravers used roman capitals with more or less italicized lower-case letters. Saxton maps have beautiful scripts, the title in italicized capitals, the serifs elaborately flourished in keeping with their setting of ornamental cartouche: excessive flourishes were part of the Dutch indulgence in baroque magnificence.

Speed used boldly rounded roman capitals, large upright lower-case type for large towns with small light italics for lesser names. Italics continued most popular through the 17th century but tended to lose their early flowing grace. This script was widely used too with roman capitals through the 18th century. But by then the English style of handwriting was becoming fashionable among the vast numbers of clerks employed throughout western Europe and this was reflected in a somewhat more flowing script with rounded capitals, used for contrast with heavy upright letters of print type. The German style of Gothic lettering returned to a small extent to English titles with the arrival of the Hanoverians when hollow letters might be used for contrast and emphasis. As might be expected engravers tended to display their lettering skill to the full on titles, sometimes including as many as a dozen forms of script in as many lines and so of course losing the very emphasis they wished for.

Most collectors, however, turn a more critical eye to the content of a map and here it is hard to look, as contemporaneous map-readers looked, for factual, accurate information. Many favourites today must have been infuriating to the man of their time, especially when old copper plates were refurbished and old errors repeated down the years. Even as late as the 1750s the Society of Arts considered it necessary to offer an annual award for a map of any English county scaled at 1 inch to the mile and accurate.

It is interesting to trace the changes in the symbols used by the old map-engravers. Mountains changed from the little hummocks used by Saxton and his contemporaries to the more angular hills of the 17th century which suggested viewing from a height so that they no longer obscured their surroundings. Speed, for example, adopted the long-enduring notion of shading the eastern side of his hills. These were followed from about 1680 by hills viewed like the rest of the map from directly overhead. Shading composed of vertical lines that would give some idea of the mountain's contours was used by John Rocque, but then he was ahead of many of his contemporaries—marking his churches by simple crosses, for example, and showing his great houses by their ground plans instead of conventionalized elevations. The "hairy caterpillar" mountain ranges were evolved in the later 18th century. Not until the second half of the 19th century did map-makers apply to their mountains the contour lines introduced far earlier on some charts of the sea.

This idea of a bird's-eye or slanting view rather than a logical view from directly overhead was used with delightful effect to show sea coasts from Armada days, not for prettiness but because it was essential on the charts used by mariners to recognize foreign shores: flags might tell them the nationalities involved so that they could approach or steer clear. Unattractive lines of hatching offered a simpler alternative for the coast during the 16th century and again in the 18th.

Speed used the bird's-eye view for the fences and trees of his parks and the method lent itself in many early maps to the presentation of what therefore appeared to be vast townships. The city castle as the dominant feature was replaced by the church for the conventionalized town symbol early in the 16th century, but the symbols were far from uniform until the 18th century and few cartographers were as meticulous as Ogilby in offering a key to his representations of cities, shire towns, corporations, market towns, cinque ports and the rest. In one of his commentaries he differentiated between capital cities shown in plan and his prospect views of "Lesser Towns and Villages, Castles, Churches, Mills, Beacons, Woods &c.". Towns long continued to be coloured red, remnant of the early roof colouring that must have appeared welcome splashes of prospective warmth and welcome to the early traveller among those endless hummocky hills.

The tower and circle customarily marking a small town in the 18th century was reduced to a simple circle by 1800. Some of these 18th-century maps—by Bowen for example—

are particularly intriguing because by then every kind of detail might be included, interpreted from its appropriate symbol. These may include post roads and their staging points (coachman's whip), rectories (R), vicarages (V), Parliamentary boroughs (stars), bishoprics, spas and so on. By the mid 18th century even woods had become masses of foliage viewed from above instead of the individual trees with east-pointing shadows that had been adopted from estate maps.

Representations of the sea changed too. Early seas, perilously turbulent, were followed by close horizontal lines of shading along the coast. Saxton used such lines, filling the rest of the sea with the regular stippling that was popular from about 1550 and only became rough water around ships and the whales, seals, porpoises and other monsters of the deep. On a Speed map an engraver might introduce the Flemish convention of staggered parallel lines suggesting "watered silk". After about 1660 the sea might be left plain but 18th-century maps from the 1730s show delicate lines closely following the outlines of the shore, and this is noted, too, in 19th-century work, although for a time late in the 18th century heavy lines of hatching came back into favour, always unattractive, whether coloured or plain.

The right colouring on maps is such a delight that it makes the many modern water-coloured imitations seem all the more deplorable. Some collectors spurn all coloured maps but this is loss as well as gain. From the 16th century they could be bought plain or individually hand coloured but for clarity the 18th century tended to prefer the colour restricted to boundaries and borders.

It is impossible to describe the quality of these old paints used in flat, transparent washes yet with a sense of substance or body to them partly due to blending with gum water. Colouring was wholly conventional, of course. Red lead was a favourite, used for rooftops and subsequently for town symbols. An unfading copper-toned green coloured with verdigris appeared in woodlands. Mountains were stone-coloured from tincture of myrrh, or umber brown and red, or a yellow-green. Other colours included gamboge (yellow), indigo, blue bice, carmine, vermillion. It must be stressed that like so much indifferently executed colouring of earlier centuries this was done by hand at a pace that would make it commercially profitable and often enough by small children—the lucky ones. Only in maps produced by lithography was the colour printed and as far as maps are concerned this was a gradual 19th-century development, easily distinguished from hand painting.

Early treatises were largely concerned with preparing the actual colours but on later maps at least if the technique was often poor it was not for want of available instruction. Even a boundary line had its own required method of approach. With brushes composed of camel hair—still the finest where a perfect point is required—held in duck quills the colourist delineated it richly along the edge and softened off with a clean damp brush on the inner side so that it would "grow faint and lose itself by degrees" as described by John Smith in the late 17th century. Smith tells in detail how to colour woods with grass-green—copper green mixed with gamboge—the sea with indigo, ships umber with sails of stone-toned tincture of myrrh, their flags vermillion or blue bice, their gunfire red lead and their smoke thinned blue bice. But mainly he is concerned with the colourists' most imaginative work that would make all the difference to the title ornament. He describes the colours for people's faces, hair, shaded costumes, for clouds, for trees that had to be in different tones of green and brown, for houses —in red lead with tiled or slated roofs in vermillion or blue bice—for castles, for blue spires and pinnacles.

The other aid to the map collector is the watermark that may be seen in the substance of the paper when it is held against the light. This was introduced in the course of making the paper so that at best it indicates only when the paper was made and not the exact date of the map itself but is often a final corroboration of a collector's deductions. At best the identification of old maps is a complex problem, however, and no detail more puzzling than their watermarks. Any collector seriously studying the subject must consult such authorities as Edward Heawood's *Watermarks of the 17th and 18th Centuries*.

Even after paper mills were established in Elizabethan

England early map-makers sought suitable paper abroad. Some of Saxton's maps are printed on French paper watermarked with bunches of grapes, sometimes stalked and topped with the initials AF. When his *Atlas of the Counties of England and Wales* was re-issued by Philip Lea in 1689 French paper was still used, showing one of the several watermarks representing the country's arms. Other French watermarks that have been noted on English maps of the 16th century include crossed arrows, a hand with a star, a tall vase or lily-pot which was common also on paper used in the 17th century and on English paper, too. The grapes and the fleur de lis continued among popular marks on French papers of the 17th and 18th centuries; the date 1742 was used on French papers for some thirty years. The fleur de lis is especially bewildering. It was long popular, too, in Italy. The 1616 issue of Speed's *Theatre* shows it with shaded petals—thought to be an English version. It appears, too, in the paper of Blome's *England*, 1671, Well's *New Sett of Maps*, 1700, Senex's *General Atlas*, 1721, and Rocque's *London*, 1746.

Indeterminate coats of arms, often with papermakers' initials and sometimes with dates, watermarked typical English map paper until the mid 18th century. Adaptations of the Amsterdam coat of arms—popular, too, in Holland from the 1660s—and the Strasbourg coat of arms were often used, too, the latter for Webb's re-issue of Saxton, 1645, Moore's map of the Fens, 1650, Speed's *Theatre*, 1676 edition, and Petty's *Ireland* 1685 and 1730. Other long-popular marks found in English maps include an eagle displayed and a horn on a shield surmounted by a crown; 18th-century marks include more versions of the fleur de lis, the arms of the City of London, a coiled serpent and the fool's cap which was popular, too, in Holland.

A conspicuous Dutch mark of the 18th century was the lion within a fence in an elaborate design under the words *pro patria*. Monogram watermarks, it seems, date from as late as about 1660 onwards but continued at least until the 1770s. Those with cursive letters date from about 1750 onwards. These details offer no more than a few clues to this difficult subject, a few glimpses into the fantastic new world of queer little men and animals, cryptic letters, pseudo-heraldry, flowers, towers, coronets that may be found when paper is examined in this way. But that is ever the way of things for those who will pause and take a second look and uncover limitless sources of intriguing and companionable treasures in the workaday, homely world of yesterday.

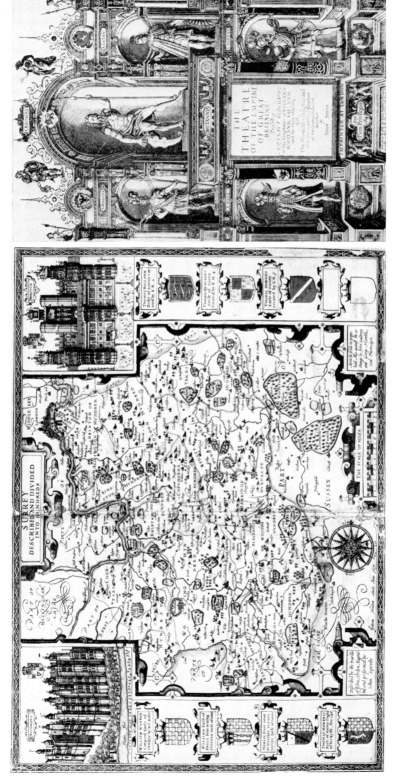

47. *Left*: magnificent views of "Richmont" and Nonsuch on a map of Surrey by John Speed, 1614, based on the journeys of John Norden. *Right*: title page from John Speed's atlas entitled *The Theatre of the Empire of Great Britaine*. The figure of "A Britaine" is flanked by a Roman and a Saxon with a Dane and a Norman below, the whole page being richly coloured and gilded.

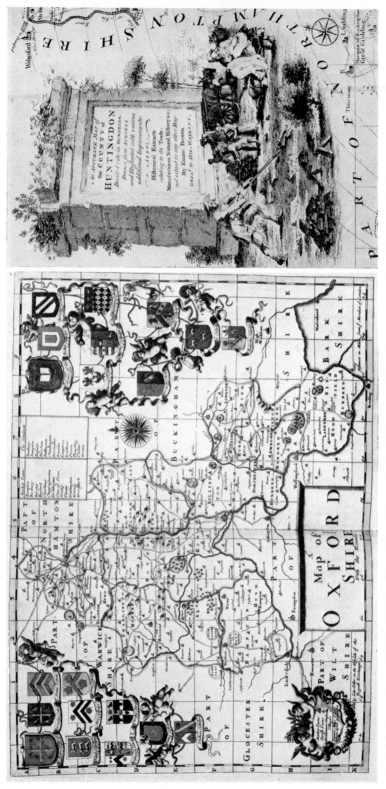

48. *Left:* early road map of Oxfordshire by John Seller, 1680, enriched with the arms of the university and various colleges. At the bottom more winged putti hold corn and fruit over a key to the symbols used for market towns, parish towns, villages and gentlemen's houses. *Right:* detail from a county map of Huntingdon by Emanuel Bowen, showing the processes of peat cutting.

Index